LIVERPOOL
THE GUIDE 04/05

Welcome

Contents

006	A Liverpool thing
017	Architecture
029	Waterfront
037	Parks and gardens
045	Walk this way
049	Pier Head and Albert Dock
057	Business District
065	Shopping Centre
075	Cultural Quarter
083	Rope Walks
089	Hope Quarter
101	World in one city
109	Hotels
123	Restaurants
141	Bars and clubs
153	Shops
165	Arts and culture
179	Entertainment
189	Sport
195	Out of town
199	Details
221	Index

Editor
■ David Cottrell
Art Director
■ Christopher Abram
Product Manager
■ Cathryn O'Grady
Research & Development
■ Jane Johnson
Sponsorship Manager
■ Jason Doherty
Advertising Sales
■ Zoe Wallace

Thanks to...
■ Stephanie Jones (contributor, fashion and Details), Tracy Sucksmith and Colin Harrison (production), Rick Cook (marketing), Phil Breen (advertising sales), Fred O'Brien (endeavour) and Ruth Hobbins (Central Library). Images of old Liverpool courtesy of the Project P.O.O.L. CD-Rom available from the Record Office, 4th Floor Central Library, priced £15.
Dave thanks his family, everyone who made the effort and Richard Starkey for setting fire to the settee.
Chris thanks R Si, Kee and Rache, with special thanks to Tiger Lily Jonswano and Emerald Luigi Jonswano.

■ A Soft Joe Production
Published by:
Trinity Mirror Merseyside

A) Trinity Mirror business

Distribution:
Orca Booksellers
Printers:
Garnett Dickinson Print Ltd

The city in one book...

■ Congratulations. Whether you're Liverpool born-and-bred or one of its two million annual visitors, you've just found the only guide to this spectacular city that matters. Some things may have changed by the time you read this – such is the pace at which Liverpool is transforming itself – but you won't find a more up-to-date, comprehensive companion to the 2008 European Capital of Culture. This is the real deal, written and produced by native Liverpudlians who know the score. Welcome to a city reborn, exciting and inspiring, and the only one (to our knowledge) with statues of Michelangelo, the Duke of Wellington, Christopher Columbus and Billy Fury. Have fun...

Message from the sponsor...
■ Vivienne Westwood found the perfect match when we opened our new boutique in Liverpool in 2003 – and we're delighted to be associated with a world-class city undergoing such a thrilling renaissance. Together we'll continue setting the trends.

A-Z of Liverpool 04/05

A is for Aintree – world-class stage for the world's greatest steeplechase.

B is for Biennial of Contemporary Art – a third in 2004, anything Venice, Berlin, Sao Paulo and Tokyo can do. And for Beetham – name of the dizzying Tower and stylish Plaza.

C is for Creamfields – dancing till the sun comes up. And Comedy – now a festival every year. And Cruise Terminal – all-new Mersey landing stage coming this way soon. And Cathedrals – the Anglican's just turned 100.

D is for Duke's Terrace – Liverpool's last back-to-back artisan dwellings, lovingly restoring.

E is for East Village – Manhattan on the Mersey. And for European Capital of Culture 2008 – we just like the sound.

F is for Films – in fact the most filmed city outside London. And for FACT – if you like your visual arts zinc-coated. And Fourth Grace – bound to cause a stir. And Football – two world-famous clubs. And Fashion – you'll soon see what we mean.

G is for Golf – choose from 40 top courses, and remember Royal Birkdale's got the Open in 2008. And for Garlands – where pretty much anything goes.

H is for Hotels – five-star fancies like the Radisson SAS, and boutique beauties like Hope Street. Staying in Liverpool just became even more fun.

I is for International – we're talking music festivals, sporting tournaments and art exhibitions. For starters.

J is for John Lennon – JLA for short, fastest-growing regional airport and first to open outside London (in 1933) – with whom it's regained its direct link. Check-in now five times a day for City Airport.

K is for King's Waterfront – next stage in the docklands renaissance, Arena and Conference Centre coming soon in a stunning location near Albert Dock.

L is for LIPA – Macca's answer to Fame, where they all learn how to fly. And for Liver Birds – look closely, you'll find them everywhere. Exempt from classification.

M is for Met Quarter – new shopping gallery gearing up for Armani. And for Marina – just the place to park your yacht. And Memphis – twinned with Liverpool in 2003

N is for Newington – funky new residential tower set to stretch over Bold Street. And for Newz Bar – glammed-up guys and gals only.

O is for **Observatory** – shaped like a lantern and home to Liverpool Vision, go see what's on.

P is for **Paradise** – biggest shopping development in Europe, on an estate the size of Mayfair. And for **Pall Mall** – executive penthouses in wine and red brick. And **Pan Am** – possibly the coolest bar in town. And **Penelope** – curves in all the right places at the old home of Cream.

Q is for **Quarter** – constantly evolving, always surprising. And something about **Queen's Dock**.

R is for **Rope Walks** – constantly evolving, always surprising Where all the ships rigging used to come from, now a cosmopolitan quarter for the creative types.

S is for **Sushi** – Sapporo Teppanyaki and the fine-art of theatre-cooking. And for **Shopping** – so many places to flash the cash. And **Spas** – soothing massage once you're through. And **Students** – over 50,000 at the last count.

T is for **Theatre** – Liverpool's Everyman and Playhouse firmly back on the map. And for **Tate** – down on Albert Dock, only London can boast more modern art. And **Trams** – £225million system coming soon, hop off and onto a canal boat down at the Pier Head.

U is for **Unity** – two new towers near the waterfront, nice views of the Liver Building. And for **UNESCO** – World Heritage Site status proposed for world-famous waterfront, 'supreme example of a maritime mercantile city'.

V is for **Vivienne Westwood** – welcome to the most glamorous store in the city. And **Vision** – the people with the plans, driving Liverpool's 21st Century renaissance.

W is for **World Discovery Centre** – seven miles of archives online in a £40million project. And for **Williamson Tunnels** – going underground with a Victorian eccentric, tunnels newly-opened off Smithdown Road.

X is for **X-Building** – floor-to-ceiling windows in funky new flats. You can see the river from here. And the pub, probably.

Y is for **Yellow Submarine** – opposite Albert Dock, as if you can miss it. And for **Yellow Duckmarine** – hour-long trips and splashdowns, too, in the groovy converted landing vehicle.

Z is for **Ziba** – seared scallops or crab-and-cauliflower gateau? Racquet Club's Modern British cuisine served all day, in the place where the A-list reside when they're paying a visit.

A Liverpool thing

Step right this way

Or hop aboard, the choice is yours...

■ You've done the Cavern, Mathew Street, Eleanor Rigby and Yellow Submarine. You've sampled the Grapes and Jacaranda, wandered around the Beatles Story (with the piano upon which John composed Imagine), even snapped the Lennon statue at the airport, and you're patiently waiting for the first volume of Mark Lewisohn's definitive Beatles history, released in 2008. Everything on your Beatles map (free from the city's Tourist Centres) is ticked off. But no trip to Liverpool is complete without a detour to Mendips and 20 Forthlin Road, the childhood homes of Lennon and McCartney. They're open from 27 March to 31 October and there's a combined minibus tour from the Albert Dock.

Worth remembering, too, that City Sightseeing is operating a new open-top, hour-long bus tour with a 24-hour, hop-on, hop-off service. You'll find details about all of Liverpool's walks and tours at the back of this book.

5 random facts

■ Liverpudlian pop artist Dave White has acquired world renown with his oil paintings of Adidas and Nike trainers, which hang on the walls of the world's hippest galleries and are soon to grace T-shirts by streetwear label One True Saxon.

■ 'A dirty, ragged, black-haired child; big enough both to walk and talk...yet when it was set on its feet, it only stared round, and repeated over and over again some gibberish that nobody could understand... The master tried to explain the matter... a tale of his seeing it starving, and houseless, and as good as dumb, in the streets of Liverpool, where he picked it up and inquired for its owner. Not a soul knew to whom it belonged, he said; and his money and time being both limited, he thought it better to take it home with him at once'... Heathcliffe enters the world's consciousness, in Emily Bronte's Wuthering Heights.

■ The perfect pan of Scouse requires a pound of diced shin-beef, chopped onion and carrots, all lobbed into a pan and simmered for three-quarters of an hour before the addition of potatoes and more boiling water. Serve hot with pickled beetroot and, if you're feeling continental, a French stick. Oo la-la, la...

■ John Moores University's Liverpool Telescope is the largest and most sophisticated robotic research telescope ever built. But you've got to go to La Palma in the Canary Islands to see it.

■ In 1982, onboard a Mersey ferry, Barbra Streisand held the second longest note in movie history in 'A Piece of Sky', the rousing finale to Yentl.

Cosmic Scouse: a bluffer's guide

■ Mersey mysticism. Scouse psychedelica. It's in the air and the water and even under the streets. Lay the blame at the telescopic lens of Jeremiah Horrocks, who in 1639 predicted the transit of Venus between the Earth and the sun (on 8 June 2004, you might recall, it happened again). His digs? Deep in the heart of Toxteth. He also discovered the moon's gravitational pull – well, the Mersey does have the second-highest tidal range in the country and now there's talk of building a massive, tidal-powered lunar clock on its banks.

This may explain why Liverpudlians are convinced there's something happening here. It can't help when a psychologist like Carl Jung dreams about the city having a tree on a little island blazing with sunlight, calls it 'a vision of unearthly beauty' and declares that Liverpool is 'the pool of life'. Goodbye city, hello state-of-mind.

Next thing you know, it's Tonight at Noon and there's a BBC TV documentary at the home of by far the greatest football team. Not to watch the match but to study the 'rhythmic swaying and singing' of the fans, 'mysteriously in touch with the spirit of Scouse'. Just then, the best band in the world release a concept album with no breaks between the tracks, Sgt Pepper for short, and John Lennon writes 'This is not here' on the windows of his house. And there's semolina pilchard climbing up the Eiffel Tower. Tatty-filarious or discomknockerating? Hard to call.

By the early 80s, collective hypsteria kicks in. Kids listen to Floyd, Hendrix, Zappa and Zeppelin. Pop stars think (i) there's an ancient spring below a manhole cover on Mathew Street; (ii) a ley-line runs directly under Liverpool, from Iceland to New Guinea. And in the 90s the lead singer of The La's declares, "The pool is where we have to be, the Liver-pool, the Mississippi, the Mersey-sippi" before sprinkling dust from vintage amps on his guitar and vanishing.

It could be the birds – you won't find them in any book of ornithology. But perhaps it's really the man with the beard who plays the cardboard ukelele outside Flanaghan's. He has a limited number of cassettes for sale, also made from cardboard. Hmm.

Get your coat
What all that heraldry means...

■ The official description of Liverpool's coat of arms...
'The Dexter Neptune, with his sea green mantle flowing, the waist wreathed with Laver; on his head an Eastern crown gold; in the right hand his trident sable; the left supporting a banner of the arms of Liverpool; on the sinister a triton, wreathed as the dexter, and blowing his shell; the right hand supporting a banner, thereon a ship under sail in perspective all proper the banner-staves Or. 'Argent, a Cormorant, in the beak a branch of seaweed called Laver, and, for the Crest, on a wreath of the colours, a Cormorant, the wings elevated, in the beak a branch of Laver; the motto is Deus Nobis Haec Otia Fecit'. (These gifts God has bestowed upon us.)

5 more random facts

■ St George's Hall is supposed to be haunted. So is the old Cotton Exchnage on Old Hall Street, where tobacco smoke is often smelled down in the vaults. And the Philharmonic Hall's 'White Lady' was first seen in 1940, telling the housekeeper that her son was safe after a wartime battle in Crete (she subsequently discovered he'd been taken prisoner, unharmed).

■ Liverpudlian Simon Rattle will return to the city in 2008 to conduct its Philharmonic Orchestra. And supermodel Jodie Kidd is a Liverpool FC fan.

■ In 1891 William F Cody, alias Buffalo Bill, travelled from New York to Liverpool in 1891 with his Wild West Show. Ten years later outlaw Butch Cassidy came out of hiding in New York, split from the Sundance Kid and sailed to Liverpool before 'retiring' to a ranch in Argentina.

■ "Liverpool is beyond questions one of the great cities of the world, and 21st Century Liverpool is undergoing an extraordinary period of development that will change the way it looks forever." Sir Neil Cossons, chairman of English Heritage, says that.

■ "Maritime commerce brought Liverpool not just wealth and employment, but also an air of cosmopolitanism that few cities in the world could rival, and it still has that sense about it. In Liverpool you still feel like you are some place." And Bill Bryson, travel writer, says that.

A Liverpool thing   010

Blairt alert!

Or how to get by in Scouse...

■ The kip of you (one's demeanour elicits dismay), ya beaut/Ted (fashion victim). Get that bifter (cigarette) out your grid (mouth), do one up the dancers (go upstairs) and give those kecks the swerve (change your trousers). Don't get airyated (exasperated) – you've had a cob/weed on (been rancorous) ever since that ardfaced mare (rude woman) behind our spec (vantage point) told you to mind yer bullet (desist from blocking her view) at the match. Her and that blairt/golfball/whopper (buffoon) were made-up (euphoric) when we made an early dart (exited the stadium prematurely). I'm dead-beat (exhausted). Let's sack off (decline) giving it toes (running for the bus and gerra joey (hail a taxi) downtown (to the city-centre). Mind that jigger-rabbit (stray cat), Ace (driver) – it's a head-the-ball (reckless thing). Yiz brewstered (credit-worthy)? Hard lines (bad luck) – it's four nicker (pounds), ya door-hinge (parsimonous wretch) so touch for that (serves you right). We'll get some scran (bite to eat) then a jar (drink) in the Big House (Vines) and have a deck at (inspect) that new alehouse. The judy (girl) behind the bar's a case (engaging character) and the owl fella (mature gentleman) on the door's a good skin (personable individual) for a wool (not native to Liverpool). Sound (how marvellous), la (old bean)...

A Liverpool thing

Getaway car.

For the first time ever, there is a Jaguar Estate car.
With either a 2 litre diesel or petrol engine and traction control.
Or 2.5 and 3 litre petrol engines with 'Traction 4' four-wheel-drive.
With the largest useable load space in its class,
it's perfect for the supermarket run or St Moritz.
For more information call 0800 70 80 60 or visit jaguar.co.uk

X-TYPE ESTATE

Born to perform

Range starts from £21,165. Car shown is 2.5 litre V6 Sport with metallic paint and silver roof rails at £26,915. Fuel economy figures for X-TYPE Esta range mpg (l/100 km). Urban 36.7 (7.7)-18.5 (15.2), extra urban 60.4 (4.7)-35.9 (7.9), combined 48.7 (5.8)-26.6 (10.6), CO_2 emissions 154-254 g/kr

If you're here in 2004...
A calender and checklist for the Year of Faith in One City

August
■ Liverpool International Beatles Week – the world's biggest annual Fab Four party, with tribute bands, guest speakers and all manner of memorabilia auctions over six days climaxing with the massive Mathew Street Festival.
■ Slavery Remembrance Day (23 Aug) – marking International Day for the Slave Trade and its Abolition. On this day back in 1791 African slaves in Haiti, Spain's first colony in Latin America, began the uprising led by Toussaint L'Ouverture that would play a crucial role in their eventual liberation.
■ Creamfields (Summer Bank Holiday 30 Aug) – 40,000 clubbers from all over the country descend on Speke Aerodrome for the UK's foremost 24-hour outdoor dancefest (cream.co.uk/creamfields).
■ QE2 on the Mersey (30 Aug) – the mighty Cunard liner calls into port and anchors mid-river for the Bank Holiday.
■ Liverpool Echo Entertainment Awards – with a rock 'n' roll theme to celebrate Liverpool's twinning with Memphis, at City Exchange.
■ Southport Flower Show – one of the UK's largest and most famous independent floral events.

September
■ Waterfront Weekend (3 to 5 Sept) – the Phil, Marc Almond, the Farm, Jo Brand and Julian Clary in a music and comedy festival at the Pier Head.
■ Heritage Open Days (10 to 13 Sept) – free access to historic buildings not usually open to the public. Previous attractions include the Ancient Chapel of Toxteth, County Sessions House and Anglican Cathedral Oratory.
■ Third Liverpool Biennial of Contemporary Art (18 Sept to 28 Nov) – a 10-week celebration of the

freshest and most innovative aspects of visual culture. Featuring the International (specially-commissioned works from around the world), the Independent (a celebration of eclectic works by acclaimed local, British and international artists), the John Moores 22 (the UK's largest contemporary painting competition – Pulp star Jarvis Cocker helped compile this year's shortlist) and the Bloomberg New Contemporaries (graduate artist showcase). Engage, enjoy.
■ Liverpool Triathalon – the new Olympic sport and the ultimate test of mental and physical stamina, comprising three legs of swimming, cycling and running, all down at the Albert Dock.
■ European Car Free Day (22 Sept) – Liverpool's Business District becomes a pedestrian zone for 13 hours and the craft stalls, rickshaws and street entertainers move in.
■ Liverpool Waterfront Classics – three nights of sweet classical music at King's Dock.
■ Lord Street European Market – carnival of continental commerce.
■ Liverpool Food & Drink Festival (late Sept) – a week of gastronomic delights organised by ketchupp.com.
■ Southport Airshow – one of the largest events of its kind, on the town's waterfront, with aircraft of every variety on display.

October
■ Liverpool Echo Fashion Show – at City Exchange on Old Hall Street.
■ Run Liverpool – 10k international half-marathon, the biggest date in the city's athletics calendar.
■ Liverpool Irish Festival (late Oct) – four-day celebration of dance, drama, literature and music with free performances across the city.

November
■ City of Liverpool Fireworks Display (5 Nov) – rockets and sparkle set to music at King's Dock and Sefton Park.
■ International Guitar Festival – acoustic heaven at various venues.
■ Christmas Lights Switch-On – with celebrities and music to light up Liverpool city-centre this Yuletide.

December
■ Festival of Light – spectacular illuminations to mark the ending of Liverpool's Year of Faith in One City.
■ Liverpool Lantern Festival (early Dec) – 200 illuminated lanterns on show as part of Santa's Parade through the city streets.
■ Lord Street European Market (week before Xmas) – the crepes and foie gras are back.
■ New Year's Eve Firework Display – ringing in the new on the spotless steps of St George's Plateau.

Or coming in 2005...
Much the same thing for the Year of the Sea

Special river cruises in 2004...
- **Liverpool Bay Cruise** (twice a day, Sat 7, 14, 21 and 28 Aug and 4 Sept) – an idyllic, 90-minute trip past New Brighton and out into Liverpool Bay.
- **Glam Rock Cruise** (Fri 13 Aug and 24 Sept) – flares, feathercuts and platform shoes. Get it on.
- **Liverpool Bird Wildlife Discovery** (Wed 18 Aug and 1 Sept) – three-hour voyage run by National Museums Liverpool and the RSPB.
- **Beatles Cruise** (Fri 27 Aug and Sat 28 Aug) – coinciding with Liverpool International Beatles Week.
- **Halloween Party Cruise** (Sat 30 Oct).
- **Fireworks Cruise** (Fri 5 Nov).
- **Glam Rock Christmas** (Fri 10 and 17 Dec).
- **60s Christmas Cruise** (Sat 11 and 18 Dec) – mop-tops on, twist and shout.
- **Children's Christmas Cruise** (Sun 12 and 19 Dec) – join Santa on the Royal Daffodil sleigh for a festive treat.

January
- Merseyside Jazz Festival – organised by Merseysippi Jazz Band at the Crowne Plaza Hotel.
- Chinese New Year (late Jan) – determined by the lunar calendar first day of the first month, with special events and a street market in Chinatown.

March
- Liverpool Performing Arts Festival – 200 hours of music, speech and drama watched by 10,000 people, now in its 80th year.
- Good Friday (25 Mar) and Easter Monday (28 Mar)

April
- The Grand National – the world's greatest steeplechase, and a four-day festival back in the city thrown in for good measure.

May
- Early May Bank Holiday (2 May)
- Liverpool Women's 10k Run – 3,000 runners converge upon Sefton Park for one of the few races in which novices can rub shoulders with top-class athletes.
- Lord Street European Market
- Writing on the Wall Festival (late May) – a week-long celebration of writing, diversity, tolerance, story-telling and humour at various venues across the city. Literary theorist Noam Chomsky, no less, made a guest appearance at last year's extravaganza.
- Spring Bank Holiday (30 May)

June
- JMU Fashion Show (early June) – recent fashion and textile graduates from John Moore University parade their designs over two days at Liverpool Art School on Hope Street.
- Mersey River Festival (mid-June) – now in its 25th year, with 250,000 visitors admiring over 150 vessels (from Tall Ships to tugs) berthed at Albert, Canning and Salthouse Docks. Truly a sight not to be missed (**merseyriverfestival.co.uk**).
- Africa Oye Festival (mid-June) – a carnival of African, Caribbean and Latin music at various venues (**africaoye.com**).
- Classic Films at the Phil (late June) – a season of cult movies in the Philharmonic Hall's unique cinema setting (**liverpoolphil.com**).
- Hope Street Midsummer Festival – arts-based community festival in an inspirational part of town.
- Lord Mayor's Parade – fun and frolics through the city streets (**llmp.org**).
- Southport Jazz Festival – experience the joy of saxophony (**southportjazz.com**).

Coming up 014

Liverpool. The life. The style. Every two months. **For free.**

2008 and all that...

■ Just so you know, 2006 is Liverpool's Year of Performance (by when it also aims to be the UK's City of Light with 30 key buildings spectacularly illuminated). Then it's 2007, the Year of Heritage and Liverpool's 800th birthday, 2008 European Capital of Culture, 2009 the Year of City Life, and 2010 the Year of Creativity and Innovation.

Fast-forward to the biggie, 2008. This promises to be Europe's biggest and most diverse celebration of culture with more than 50 international festivals scheduled. Among the highlights will be: the first-ever showing in Europe of the treasures of the Chinese Xia dynasty; the grand openings of Will Alsop's Fourth Grace on the waterfront and the World Discovery Centre at Central Library on William Brown Street, linked by a brand new Archive Trail running through the heart of the proposed UNESCO World Heritage Site; a brand new International Festival of Comedy and FACT International Festival of New Cinema; and, of course, the Fifth Liverpool Biennial of Contemporary Art featuring 50 leading artists from all over the globe and 10 major new commissions.

There's more. Liverpool will be host port for the start of the 2008 Tall Ships Race, with the biggest vessels berthed at the new cruise-liner terminal. It'll welcome back the yachts from the 35,000-mile Round the World Clipper Race. The Open Golf Championship will be staged at Royal Birkdale near Southport. And that's before we get to the Grand National, Beatles Week, Creamfields, Summer Pops, River Festival...

July

■ HUB Festival (3 and 4 July) – the biggest names in BMX, skate, hip-hop and graffiti hit the waterfront.
■ Liverpool Festival of Comedy (early July) – a fortnight of stand-ups and superstars (Jackie Mason last year).
■ Liverpool Summer Pops – three weeks of beautiful music in the Big Top Tent at King's Dock. Macca's played here. So have Elton, Dylan, Westlife, Busted and The Corrs.
■ Liverpool International Tennis Tournament – five days of fantastic tennis at the 5,000-seater Centre Court in Calderstones Park, with ATP players and legends mixing it before Wimbledon's first serve.
■ Liverpool International Street Festival (late July) – a week-long spectacle of dance, drama and music from all over the globe.

■ Liverpool Arabic Arts Festival (1 to 30 July) – the country's only dedicated Arabic event, with artists from Egypt, Morocco, Tunisia, Yemen, Iraq, Jordan, Palestine and Britain.

August

■ Downtown Week (15 to 22 Aug) – art, media and business in synergy.
■ Liverpool International Beatles Week/Mathew Street Festival
■ Slavery Remembrance Day (23 Aug)
■ Creamfields (29 Aug)
■ Liverpool Echo Entertainment Awards
■ Southport Flower Show

September

■ Heritage Open Days (10 to 13 Sept)
■ Liverpool Triathalon
■ European Car Free Day
■ Liverpool Waterfront Classics

■ Lord Street European Market
■ Liverpool Food & Drink Festival (late Sept)
■ Southport Airshow

October

■ Liverpool Echo Fashion Show
■ Run Liverpool
■ Liverpool Irish Festival (late Oct)

November

■ City of Liverpool Fireworks Display (5 Nov)
■ International Guitar Festival
■ Christmas Lights Switch-On

December

■ Liverpool Lantern Festival (early Dec)
■ Lord Street European Market (week before Xmas)
■ New Year's Eve Firework Display

Coming up 016

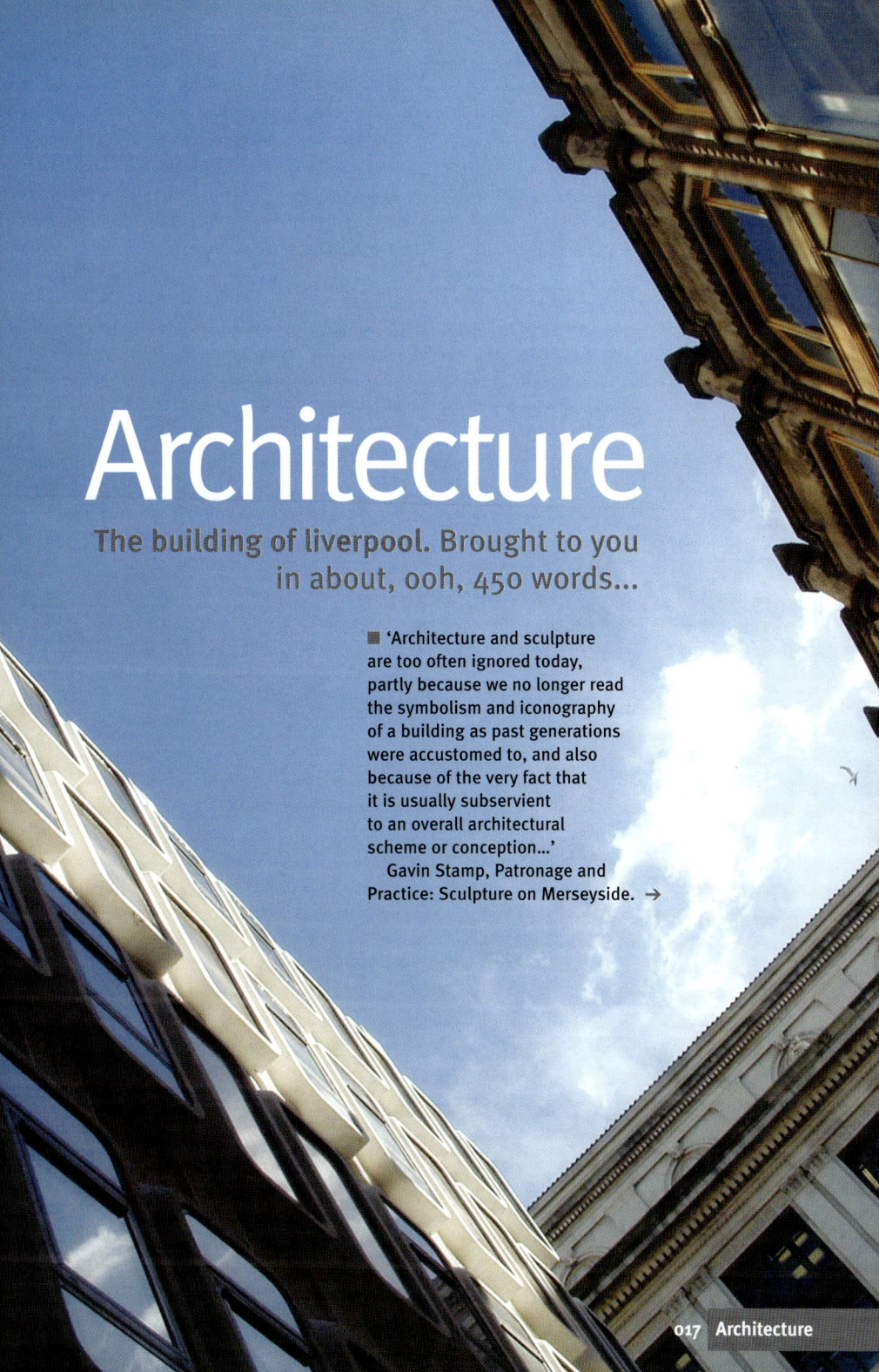

Architecture

The building of liverpool. Brought to you in about, ooh, 450 words...

■ 'Architecture and sculpture are too often ignored today, partly because we no longer read the symbolism and iconography of a building as past generations were accustomed to, and also because of the very fact that it is usually subservient to an overall architectural scheme or conception...'
Gavin Stamp, Patronage and Practice: Sculpture on Merseyside. →

Best of 3...
coats of arms

■ Compton House, Church Street. Top of Marks and Sparks, two mermen with shell for a shield, customary Liver Birds and city motto.

■ St George's Hall. In semi-circular stained glass above great organ at south end, with another depicting George and Dragon in north.

■ Mersey Travel, 24 Hatton Garden. In granite, dating from 1907. The merman on the right should always blow a conch to summon the sea.

■ Make a fortune from shipping in the 19th Century and build a world-famous city with the proceeds. Line the docks with mighty warehouses. Express your power, pride and prestige with exuberant but dignified offices, commodity exchanges and noble banks with bronze doorways, iron balconies and exquisite sculpture. And erect rows of merchant palaces on the brow.

Specialise in Greco-Roman grandeur on a scale not seen in the provinces to create an Athens of the north. Build magnificent museums, galleries and libraries like ancient temples, and entrust a 23-year-old doomed genius to design the finest neo-classical edifice in Europe.

At the turn of the next century turn your back on the capital's Victorian aesthetic and look to the New World instead. Make breakthroughs in engineering. Use steel and concrete. Build skyscrapers that occupy whole blocks. Create a skyline like the great American cities with which you do business. Put three sisters on your waterfront, each with a character of her own: from baroque and opulent, to square and disciplined, eclectic and eccentric.

Enjoy a second Greek Revival – like nowhere else in Britain – and combine classicism with abstraction, the past with the modern. Call it 'The Liverpool Manner'. Explore Art Deco. Revisit Renaissance detail. Make an Expressionist masterpiece of a three-mile hole in the ground. Make the philharmonic, acoustic.

Then hit the brakes. Watch wartime bombing wreak wholesale devastation. See containerisation cripple the port economy. No more ships and sailors, nor exciting new buildings. But no mass demolition and brutalist redevelopment, either. And when the tide begins to change, rejoice in a fabulous architectural legacy preserved in situ – and vow to complement it with a flourish of futuristic, world-class buildings.

Experience a renaissance. Go for Heritage Site status. Become Capital of Culture. Be epic and theatrical, bold and daring once more. Be Liverpool back to her best.

■ Liverpool has 2,500 listed properties, including 26 Grade I, more than any other city outside London. Buildings that qualify: (i) those before 1700 that survive in anything like their original condition; (ii) those between 1700 and 1840 subject to selection; (iii) those between 1840 and 1914 of definite quality and character. Grade I are of exceptional interest. Grade II of special interest.

Architecture

019 | Architecture

Anatomy of an art gallery

■ The Walker on William Brown Street typifies 19th-Century Liverpool's love affair with neo-classicism, combining Greek ideals of harmony with Roman advances in technology. Its portico (entrance bay) is a temple projecting from an ashlar (square-cut stone) façade. The rest is in the details...

Best of 3... doorways

■ **Caffe Nero,** Castle Street. Old Adelphi Bank. Bronze doors depicting pairs of inseparable friends: Achilles and Patroclus; Castor and Pollux; Roland and Oliver.

■ **Stanley Hall,** Edmund Street. Gleaming brass on authentic Art Deco frontage, formerly home to Silcocks grain merchants.

■ **National Provincial Bank,** Water Street. Ferocious tigers whose fangs were ritually rubbed by Indian sailors for good luck.

■ **Pediment:** triangular roof surmounting the portico, with tympanum (often featuring reliefs or busts) at its centre.

■ **Cornice:** horizontal decorative projection, here running along pediment and crowning entablature.

■ **Entablature:** upper part of portico or entrance bay, supported by columns and including cornice.

■ **Capital:** stylised elaboration at top of column, typically acanthus leaves (spiky shrub common in Mediterranean countries).

■ **Shaft:** slender part of column.

■ **Pedestal:** plinth and dado (square slab) supporting base of column.

■ **Frieze:** horizontal band of decorative sculpture along walls of façade.

■ **Corinthian column:** one of five types of classical column, with fluted shaft and decorated capital, and used by Romans. The other four are: Doric (simplest Greek order – see Wellington's Column); Ionic (Greek with scrolls either side of capital – see Oratory next to Anglican Cathedral); Tuscan (least ornamented); and Composite (mixing Corinthian and Ionic).

Architecture

The neo-classical Church of St Bride on Percy Street (Hope Quarter)

021 Architecture

Sun and moon and stars, high above Anderson's Bar on Exchange Street East

Best of 3... mosaics

■ **Walls of Reliance House,** Tower Gardens (off Water Street). Panel of ancient and modern ships salvaged from Colonial House, which was bombed by Luftwaffe in May 1941.

■ **Floor of Albion House,** James Street. Map of South America in erstwhile head-quarters of White Star Shipping Line.

■ **Reservation outside Queensway Tunnel,** Old Haymarket. Map with blue-and-yellow Liver Bird, celebrating Tunnel's ceremonial opening in 1934.

Four of a kind

■ Some of the most beautiful Victorian offices in Liverpool's Business District were designed by James Picton (1805-89). The Central Library's Reading Room on William Brown Street (Cultural Quarter) was named after this prolific architect who was knighted for his services to the city. Inspired by the architecture of Venetian palaces, his buildings are characterised by strong façades with heavy cornices, and round-arched windows with granite columns, rope mouldings and reliefs. The apotheosis of his style is probably the Hargreaves Building on Chapel Street, now home to the Racquet Club (see Hotels). It was built for William Brown himself, the wealthy cotton merchant and MP, and above the windows are busts of famous explorers plus the Spanish king and queen Ferdinand and Isabella. Pictured above (clockwise from top left): 11 Dale Street; Fowler's Building on Victoria Street; Hargreaves Building on Chapel Street; and 48 Castle Street.

Building the Liver Building

Best of 3... Neptunes

■ **Former College of Commerce,** Tithebarn Street. Feisty figurehead looming over ship's prow above what's now part of John Moores University.

■ **Martins Bank Building,** Water Street. Dolphins either side of his bald head and Assyrian beard and his webbed fingers upon heads of two boys.

■ **Cotton Exchange,** Old Hall Street. Colossal Mersey statue clasping anchor, tiller and rope and pouring water over dolphin.

■ In 1911 Pablo Picasso was in Paris, painting objects as he thought them. In New York a waiter called Berlin was composing Alexander's Ragtime Band, while Amundsen was heading for the South Pole and the town of Caernarfon had invested a new Prince of Wales.

In Liverpool construction of the Anglican Cathedral moved into its 10th year as over 35million tons of shipping entered and left the port annually. And the Royal Liver Insurance Company unveiled its new home on the site of the old George's Dock (filled in with cotton bales to soak up residual water). It was reported by the Liverpool Weekly Mercury as 'a gigantic structure' and hailed as Europe's first skyscraper.

The architect Walter Aubrey Thomas ignored an original plan to design a similar structure to the Port of Liverpool Building (completed four years earlier) and drew heavily on the new American style of multi-storeyed rows of identical windows, bays and pilasters stacking skywards. He also copied the US practice of shared entrances, lifts and washrooms for all employees.

His towering vision was made possible, though, by an innovation from France. A decade earlier Louis Mouchel had arrived in Britain with a licence to use the new technique of reinforcing concrete with iron bars. Under his guidance in Liverpool, the builders Nuttal & Co erected a giant frame composed of hundreds of ferro-concrete 'ribs' (beams and columns) that carried loads of up to 1,500 tons and held together an 320ft high, 11-floor block. There were 483 steps to the domed clock towers (middle pic shows Liver staff dining on one of the faces) whose copper birds were made in Bromsgrove and re-assembled in Liverpool.

On 19 July 1911, three years after Lord Stanley laid its foundation stone, the most imposing example of ferro-concrete in the world was open for business.

Architecture 024

All lit up

025 **Architecture**

Let there be light

Best of 3... domes

■ **Town Hall,** Castle Street. Dizzyingly beautiful blue, white and gold decoration inside, with city motto and history of building in large gilded letters along the base.

■ **Port of Liverpool Building,** Pier Head. You shouldn't really stick one on top of Renaissance palace. But who cares? Glorious.

■ **Lyceum Building,** Bold Street. Sub-Sistine splendour for diners in Prohibition's restaurant, formerly home to Post Office.

■ Walk down Princes Street in the Business District, hang a right down Roe Alley towards North John Street and you might think you've been transported to the Middle East – or at least the set of Indiana Jones & The Last Crusade. There, ahead of you and framed by the alley's gorge-like walls, is Liverpool's equivalent of the temple at Petra, the wonder of the ancient world hewn from the pink cliffs of the desert.

Except this isn't Jordanian rock, it's Portland Stone – cladding two of the six great ventilation shafts designed by Herbert Rowse for the Queensway Tunnel in the 1930s, and used for several other fine buildings in the city as well as St Paul's Cathedral in London.

Quarried for centuries from the eponymous peninsula in Dorset, it's a 200million-year-old limestone composed of fossilised shell creatures and famous for its capacity to absorb and reflect light. Carving it – say the experts – is like cutting into a block of light, creating darkness with each cut of the chisel and even producing rhythmic sound waves through its brittle granular structure. A simple, stunningly beautiful building material, as our Indy would no doubt agree.

Architecture 026

Brick version of the ventilation shaft, on Rumford Street

027 Architecture

The best views are not always out of the window

The European Capital of Culture 2008 now has a hotel which reflects such an accolade. Stunning interiors and rooms effortlessly combining contemporary style and comfort. With an enticing choice of ways to relax and unwind including the sumptuous Filini restaurant and the chic "White Bar" lounge and cocktail bar make the Radisson SAS your only choice. Then there's the impressively equipped Ark Health and Fitness Club which boasts an indoor swimming pool, jacuzzi, sauna, gymnasium, dance studio and beauty treatment rooms. If you still have time for work, there's a dedicated meeting and event floor, offering nine conference rooms, complete with all the technical facilities you can think of. And one or two you might not.

Radisson SAS Hotel
107 Old Hall Street, Liverpool L3 9BD United Kingdom
Telephone 0151 966 1500   Facsimile 0151 966 1501
www.radissonsas.com

Waterfront

A compass reading in a city with saltwater running through its veins...

■ 'The least appreciated quality of Mersey is its physical beauty. The vast sky overhangs a fine, wide river that curves around the shoreline like a silver scimitar. There is an unsuspecting grandeur in Liverpool's setting. From a hilltop or a ferry boat you can watch the weather bearing down on you from Wales. The waterfront buildings are as magnificent as their cousins in Shanghai and Chicago'...
  Paul Du Noyer, Liverpool: Wondrous Place →

Best of 3... waterfront views

■ **Mersey Ferries.** The original and best. Go for the hour-long trip from the Pier Head to Seacombe, Woodside and back with views as far as Perch Rock.

■ **Seacombe Ferry Terminal.** Wistful views from the same point where, they say, Edward II sailed across the Mersey back in 1323.

■ **Egremont Promenade.** Further north on the Wirral coast, where the cathedrals, Royal Liver Building and Beetham Tower are still visible.

■ Amid all the parties and celebrations there's a special conference planned in Liverpool for 2008, and only Naples, Marseilles and Bilbao are invited. Called the Cities at the Edge Festival, it'll explore the creative and historic threads that connect all of these famous ports and their sense of identity shaped by the sea.

Its architecture awash with maritime symbolism (anchors, mermaids, dolphins, shells, seaweed etc), Liverpool is defined by its location, looking out and away from the rest of the country. The River Mersey, declared writer Michael O'Mahoney in 1931, "is a threshold to the ends of the earth."

Let's get our bearings. The bit that everyone knows is the Pier Head and Albert Dock, the latter now one of the UK's biggest tourist attractions with more than five million visitors. It already stages the UK jet ski championships and in 2008 this will be the setting for Europe's biggest and most ambitious laser and firework display. Here's where the Round the World Clipper Race will begin and end in 2005/06 and 2007/08, too, calling in at ports like Panama City, Shanghai, Cape Town and New York along the way. It's also the place where the biggest and most beautiful Tall Ships, from 30ft yachts to spectacular square-riggers, will berth before their race in 2008, with a new Olympic-style village for the crews.

Head south from here and you come, consecutively, to the docks of King's (where they're building an £85million Arena & Conference Centre), Wapping, Queen's, Coburg and Brunswick (home to the Liverpool Marina & Harbourside Club). All of these docks, which represent a fifth of the nominated UNESCO World Heritage Site, are currently getting a new lease of life from British Waterways with improved moorings, leisure trips and year-round watersports and maritime events.

Back to the Pier Head, set to become the ultimate Liverpool focal point for locals and visitors alike when the Fourth Grace is completed in 2007, while a new tram network and canal link converge outside and a £12million cruise-liner terminal opens just to the north at Prince's Dock near the Crowne Plaza.

Prince's Dock, which remained a working dock right up to 1981, is undergoing its own programme of massive redevelopment, its calm waters and cobblestones complemented by state-of-the-art buildings designed to absorb natural light through solar-tinted glass and open-plan atriums.

It was from here that millions of emigrants left for the New World while its cargoes came the other way.

Herman Melville, author of Moby Dick, described proceedings in his 1849 novel Redburn: 'Here lie the noble New York packets, which at home are found at the foot of Wall Street; and here also lie the Mobile and Savannah cotton ships and traders. Princes Dock is so filled with shipping that the entrance of a newcomer occasions a universal stir. The dock-masters mount the poops of the various vessels and hail the surrounding strangers in all directions: "Highlander ahoy! Cast off your bowline and sheer alongside the Neptune!" "Neptune ahoy! Get out a stern line and sheer alongside the Trident!" "Trident ahoy! Get out a bow line and drop astern of the Undaunted!" And so it runs round of electricity; touch one, and you touch all'. →

Further north now to what's confusingly called the Central Docks and comes under the aegis of the Stanley Dock Conservation Area, one of five zones comprising the World Heritage Site. As well as warehouses, they're home to the largest parabolic silo in Europe (built to house 100,000 tons of raw sugar) and a huge pumping station that bores deep into the riverbed.

Running alongside for the best part of six miles is the 200-year-old, fortress-like Dock Wall (right), rising 18ft high in places and punctuated by colossal gatepiers. The novelist Nathaniel Hawthorne, American consul in Liverpool in the 1850s, likened it to the Great Wall of China. Similarly, an overhead railway (dubbed the Docker's Umbrella) once ran the length of this area, from the Dingle to Seaforth, until its closure in 1956.

Waterloo, the first of the Central Docks, was opened in 1834 to handle grain imports from North America. Its surviving warehouse (there were three) was converted into flats in 1990 and has as much floorspace as all of the Albert Dock buildings put together. But it's still dwarfed by the gargantuan, 27million-brick Tobacco Warehouse (below) half-a-mile away at Stanley Dock – opposite which is

The Tobacco Warehouse: giant from a bygone era

Now this is what you call a wall

Tunnel vision

■ Opened in 1886, the Mersey Railway Tunnel was the first underwater railway in the world. The first road tunnel opened in 1936 and was one of the century's greatest feats of engineering. Queensway required the excavation of 1.2million tons of rock over five years. To put it another way, one ton was removed every two minutes, and for each ton of rock raised to the surface 26 tons of water were pumped to a height of 200ft. One million bolts were used, plus 270,000 tons of concrete and 82,000 tons of cast-iron to line the tunnel walls, and the average cover of rock, gravel and clay between its top and the river is 35ft. A second road tunnel, Kingsway, opened in 1971.

Collingwood Dock, through whose gates passed most of the 1,300,000 Irish migrants who fled the Famine and 'took the ship' to Liverpool around 1845-52. Upon the wall a green plaque in Celtic decorative art marks this pivotal moment in history.

After Collingwood, another great swathe of docks – Salisbury, Nelson, Bramley Moore, Wellington, Sandon, Huskisson, Canada, Brocklebank and Langton – run right up to Liverpool Freeport (the modern container terminal which absorbed the old Alexandra, Hornby, Gladstone and Royal Seaforth docks). Ripe for redevelopment now, they were a riot of commotion 150 years ago.

Melville again: 'Here are brought together the remotest limits of the earth; and in the collective spars and timbers of these ships, all the forests of the globe are represented as in a grand parliament of masts'.

Those days are gone, but the current River Festival, now running for over 20 years, must rekindle something of the scene – the Mersey packed once again with liners, ferries, pleasure-craft, sea-going yachts and historic naval vessels, and the kind of traffic congestion no-one could begrudge.

Nightfall over Prince's Dock

WATERFRONT 034

What's to do...

■ 'Everything you need for a good night's sleep, and nothing you don't'. That's the Travelodge motto, and it applies to all 250 of our hotels in the country. The en-suite rooms are spacious and comfortable, with luxury Hypnos beds, colour TV and tea and coffee-making facilties. Plus free car-parking, friendly restaurants nearby – a Little Chef, Burger King or Harry Ramsden's to choose from – and an Early Bird Breakfast delivered to your room for just £4.45. There's no check-out, either – it's all done when you arrive – and rooms cost from just £25 per room per night (bring your dog for only £5 more). You'll find Travelodge on Liverpool's Haymarket in the city-centre, and on Brunswick Dock on the waterfront, with great views of the nearby Marina. Hope to see you soon...

035 **Advertorial**

What's new

■ Between Southport and the Wirral lies 120km of coastline, much of which is internationally important for nature conservation, and £80million has been set aside to create a Mersey Waterfront Regional Park with a continuous network of walkways. The focal point is Liverpool's waterfront, which has its own unified vision incorporating several major new developments.

Will Alsop, the architect behind the Fourth Grace, has already talked of a fifth, perhaps between the Royal Liver Building and Crowne Plaza. As it is, there'll be a £12million cruise-liner terminal (middle left) in place by 2005.

The new 2.5km canal link (top left) will allow inland boats to sail from the Leeds and Liverpool Canal, through the Central Docks, past the Pier Head and into the Albert Dock. It'll include two new locks, five new bridges and a tunnel, all at a level below the Pier Head with seating close to the water and shelter from the wind.

Further south, the 'world-class development' promised for King's Dock (bottom left) will be designed by leading architects Wilkinson & Eyre, with lots of street furniture, cafés and green spaces around the proposed Arena & Conference Centre and a riverside walkway to the Albert Dock and beyond. And watch this space, possibly, for a new 50-storey tower down at Brunswick Dock, and a giant wave-powered glass-sculpture called the Aluna Project that lights up according to the phases of the moon and displays the Mersey's tidal changes.

Green and serene

Relax. In town and off the beaten park there are plenty of oases of tranquillity...

037 Parks and gardens

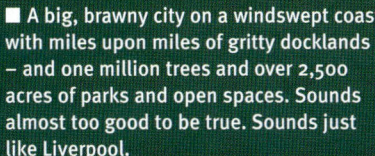

■ A big, brawny city on a windswept coast with miles upon miles of gritty docklands – and one million trees and over 2,500 acres of parks and open spaces. Sounds almost too good to be true. Sounds just like Liverpool.

The great swathes of Stanley Park and Newsham Park (both east of the city centre) and Sefton Park (to the south) are a legacy from late Victorian days when Liverpool's great and good had the foresight – in the nick of time – to create green lungs and leafy arteries for a city seething and sprawling with humanity.

For years the cherished notion had been to build a city as beautiful as Florence. A century on, Liverpudlians are beginning to appreciate again how lucky they are. Five of the city's parks are included on the English Heritage Register of Historic Parks as Grade II sites and eight have been awarded Green Flag status by the Civic Trust.

Chavasse Park, close to the waterfront, is being re-landscaped as part of the massive Paradise Street project and the city has its own National Wildflower Centre set in a tranquil park in Knowsley (just off the M62). Check out its well-stocked shop and the wonderful 160-metre rooftop walkway.

Liverpool is championing not just conservation but ecology, too. At Croxteth Hall & Country Park (north-east) a former estate has been transformed into 400 acres of woodland and farm with a Victorian walled garden. And last year the Merseyside Caribbean Centre on Parliament Street unveiled a wildflower garden containing mosaic flags of the six West Indian islands made from coloured glass chippings, to coincide with the first annual National Recycling Week.

Sefton Park, 132 years old and the grandest of all the green spaces, is awash with joggers these days and stages mass events like the annual Liverpool Women's 10k Run. But it still harbours corners of peace and quiet amid its 200 acres of mature forest trees.

Designed by local architect Louis Hornblower and Edouard André, a Parisian pupil of Napoleon III's landscape gardener, it's a fairytale landscape of curved pathways, streams with stepping stones and bridges, grottos and gateways, ornamental buildings and a boating lake. In spring, along its sweeping oval edge, there really is a host of golden daffodils, as well as carpets of brilliant bluebells.

A couple of miles east is Calderstones, now home to the Liverpool International Tennis Tournament and a 125-acre Eden named after a stone formation dating back 4,000 years. Like Sefton Park, it has its own lake and glasshouse, plus a Japanese flower garden with koi carp in a lily-covered pond. There's also a dog-free picnic area and children's playground opened by Paul McCartney in memory of his late wife Linda. The colossal figures either side of the entrance gates are Atlantes – carvings of the Titan in Greek mythology who held up the pillars of the Universe.

You can explore all of these beautiful parks with Liverpool Rangers, who offer a wide range of walks, talks and organised events, most of which are free of charge (0151 225 5710). This may be a football-mad city split down the middle between rabid Reds and loyal Blues, but there's definitely a growing army of fanatical Greens.

Story of the Palm House

■ The Grade II listed jewel in Sefton Park's crown was a gift from millionaire Henry Yates Thompson in 1896. It measures 100ft in diameter and rises 82 feet in three glazed tiers from an octagonal base of red granite from the Isle of Mull. Shattered by an incendiary bomb during the Second World War, it was painstakingly restored by a group of local residents and is once again a major botanical and events attraction.

Come home to The Living Room which has now become synonymous with excellent service and stylish surroundings across the UK. The Living Room is a neighbourhood based Restaurant and Bar focusing on casual dining.

Mosquito is an upbeat , high-energy cocktail bar/ club situated below The Living Room incorporating The Vampire Suite, Liverpool's premier private members' bar situated below Mosquito and is available for private hire.

For menus, venues, news and views visit www.thelivingroom.co.uk

The Living Room, 15 Victoria Street, Liverpool, L2 5QS
0870 44 22 535 liverpool@thelivingroom.co.uk
www.thelivingroom.co.uk

Stars of the Palm House

■ Outside are elegant statues of Christopher Columbus (the only one of its kind in Britain), James Cook, Henry the Navigator and Charles Darwin, among others. Inside are flora from five continents – just a sample from Liverpool's world-renowned botanical collection – and a date palm called Olive whose fan-shaped leaves were already stretching skywards when Queen Victoria cut the ribbons to her new home.

043 Parks and gardens

Best of 3... urban retreats

■ **Bluecoat Courtyard**, off School Lane. Rustic haven in one of Liverpool's oldest buildings, slap-bang in the middle of the Shopping Centre.

■ **St James Gardens**, Anglican Cathedral. Home to wild roses, native and exotic, like the Burnet, Abyssinia, Damask, Tibetan and Old Blush.

■ **St John's Gardens**, behind St George's Hall. Former church site in the Cultural Quarter, laid out as terraced gardens 100 years ago.

Parks and gardens

The big picture

The city-centre of Liverpool. In six easy sections...

045 Walk this way

Location key:

○ Pier Head and Albert Dock
○ Business District
○ Shopping Centre
○ Cultural Quarter
○ Rope Walks
○ Hope Quarter

N

Walk this way

■ Liverpool city-centre is easily subdivided into six walkable areas, each with their own distinct identity: the maritime Pier Head and Albert Dock, commercial and architecturally-important Business District, retail-led Shopping Centre, neo-classical Cultural Quarter, dynamic Rope Walks and idyllic Hope Quarter. Follow the trail in depth over the next 50 pages – there's a map for each area and information about local landmarks and other points of interest. Plus some rather nice pictures, we'd like to think...

047 Walk this way

Going your way in Liverpool

Whether you are sightseeing, shopping or socialising, let Arriva take you there...

Comfortably
Regularly
Safely

Ask your driver for an Arriva Day Ticket, which offers unlimited travel on our buses in the Merseyside area for only **£3.30**. Family tickets are also available for just **£7.00**.

Arriva 2008 draw
Celebrating Liverpool's Capital of Culture success.

Don't forget to check your ticket - it could win you £2008!

If the serial number on your ticket reads 2008 then send it to us. £2008 prize draws will take place every 3 months.

1. Pier Head and Albert Dock

■ What better place to start than the iconic water's edge? Top of the tourist ticklist, the Pier Head is dominated by the familiar mirages of the Royal Liverpool Building, Cunard Building and Port of Liverpool Building, today known collectively as the Graces after three daughters of Zeus who represented splendour, festivity and abundance (see John Gibson's sculpture in the Walker Gallery). A spectacular Fourth Grace, you're probably aware, is on the way. This is a wonderfully walkable area, book-ended by the exciting new developments at Prince's Dock and the myriad attractions of Albert Dock.

Walk this way

1. Pier Head and Albert Dock

The attractions...
- **ER** Engine Room Monument
- **LB** Liver Building
- **CB** Cunard Building
- **PB** Port of Liverpool Building
- **GB** George's Dock Building
- **FG** Fourth Grace Site
- **ML** Museum of Liverpool Life
- **LP** Lusitania Propeller
- **MM** Maritime Museum
- **TL** Tate Liverpool
- **BS** Beatles Story

The hotels...
- **1** Crowne Plaza
- **2** Premier Lodge
- **3** Express by Holiday Inn

The bars and restaurants...
- **1** Shanghai Palace
- **2** Est Est Est
- **3** Blue Bar & Grill
- **4** Baby Cream

The shops...
- **1** Ocean
- **2** Room Store

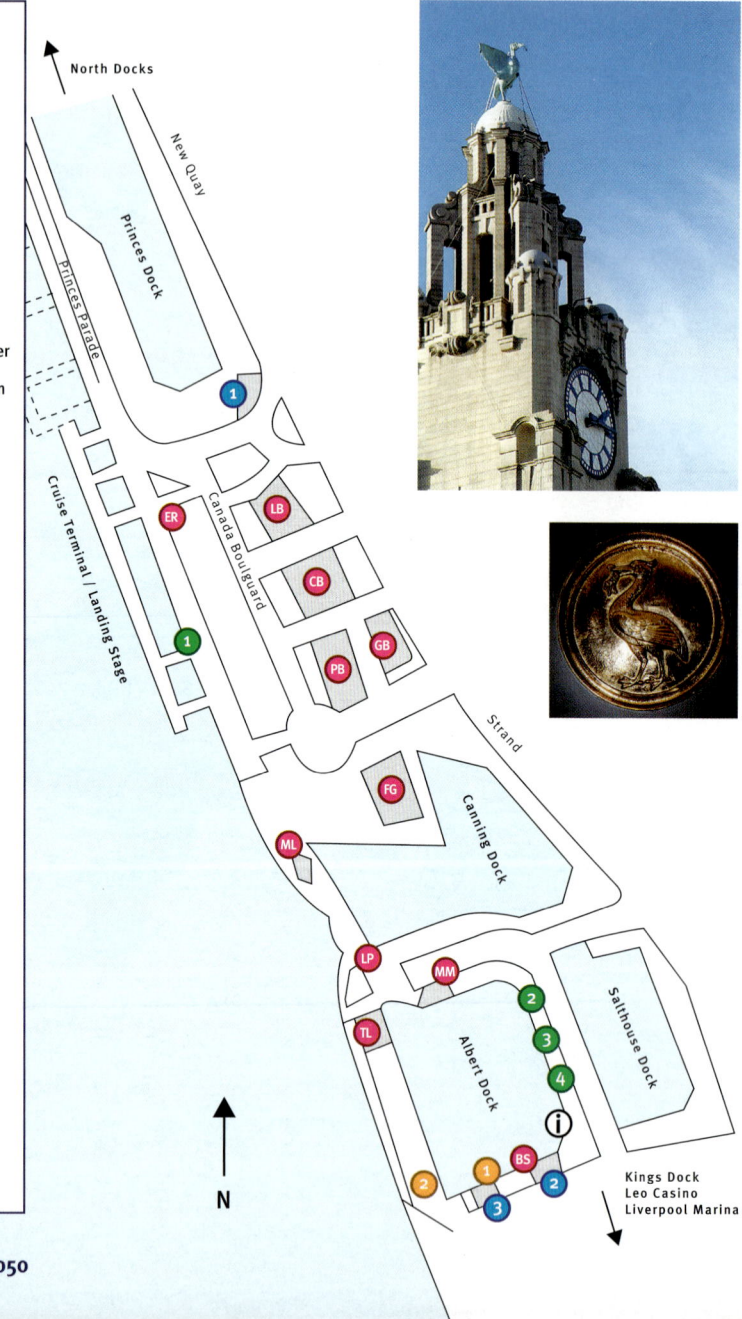

Kings Dock
Leo Casino
Liverpool Marina

Walk this way   050

Royal Liver Building

■ Grade I listed and up there with Big Ben as the most instantly recognisable building in the country. It was constructed in 1911 as the new headquarters for the Royal Liver Friendly Society and symbolises an era of industry, ingenuity and wealth (it was officially opened while the Lusitania was in port) and remained Britain's tallest building until the advent of tower blocks in the 1960s.

Designed by Walter Aubrey Thomas, the architect behind the adjacent Tower Building and the Philharmonic Hotel, its scale and style were inspired by the buildings of Chicago, a city that had arisen just as rapidly as Liverpool – although the circular entrance facing the river is actually modelled on an ancient temple at Baalbek in modern-day Lebanon.

This marvel of engineering stands 320ft high, occupies over an acre of land and weighs 80,000 tons, and the diameter of each clock face – there are four altogether – is 25ft (the largest in Britain). The great birds, made of hammered copper and standing three times as tall as man, were designed by Carl Bernard Bartels, a German craftsman who was subsequently imprisoned and forcibly repatriated during the First World War.

Inside, there are Liver Birds on the lift doors (left), and a stained glass window (above) at the western end of the recently refurbished ground floor. It features a central figure representing Navigation and Commerce, standing on a landing stage and holding a mariner's chart and caduceus (wand carried by Hermes, the messenger god), with an anchor and capstan at her feet. Below her, Neptune emerges from a shell holding a trident, and elsewhere there are sea nymphs, dolphins, boat hooks, sextants and ancient and modern ships.

It happened here...

■ Today Prince's Dock is at the hub of the waterfront renaissance and home to the Crowne Plaza Hotel, private bankers Coutts, and a proposed hotel and two residential towers with luxury apartments designed by Terence Conran. But for a century it was a conduit of world history – the departure point for nine million emigrants sailing to America from 1821 onwards. Who knows how many famous names in today's United States have ancestors that walked down its gangways?

In 1919 and today (below)

Pier Head

Old man of the sea

Cunard Building

■ The third and supposedly final Grace was completed in 1916 for Cunard, whose first ship, the Britannia, sailed from Liverpool to North America on 4 July 1840 (exactly 162 years later the keel of its latest vessel, the Queen Mary 2, was lowered into the dock at the St Nazaire shipyard in Brittany). Upon completion of Liverpool's cruise-liner terminal in 2005, Cunard is proposing to name a new 85,000-ton vessel in the shadow of its former home, which takes the form of an Italian palazzo decorated with Greek-style details of peoples from around the world. Grade II listed and, like her two sisters, built to last.

Port of Liverpool Building

■ Formerly the Mersey Docks & Harbour Board Building, it was constructed four years earlier than the Royal Liver Building and is now Grade II listed. Designed in the style of a Renaissance palace – but unusually with a classical dome at the centre – it's best described as Edwardian baroque.

The opulent interior has a mosaic floor with a compass motif (right) and rows of stained glass windows dedicated to countries of the British Empire, and the balcony above the ground floor quotes Psalm 107 in gilt letters: 'They that go down to the sea in ships that do business in great waters these see the works of the Lord and his wonders of the deep'. Epic.

Fourth Grace

■ 'Something that is totally Liverpool, totally memorable and has never been seen before'. That's how architects Alsop describe their controversial 'Cloud' vision for the Pier Head. Having seen off competition from Richard Rogers and Norman Foster to design the forthcoming Fourth Grace, they also plan to create an illuminated 'garden of light' along the waterfront, house an open-plan museum and make all four Graces 'truly public' by connecting their atriums. There's even talk of a Fifth Grace on the other side of the Liver Building. Watch this space.

Cloud. Your judgment?

George's Dock Building

■ Another Art Deco masterpiece by Herbert Rowse (see the Martins Bank Building and Philharmonic Hall), dating from 1934 and, for many, the original Fourth Grace. Its monolithic shape was inspired, some say, by Howard Carter's excavations in Egypt a decade earlier, but is there a touch of Flash Gordon about the futuristic details?

At the base are two figures in black basalt symbolising Night and Day, and all four sides of the central shaft of the building feature decorative panels flanked by sculptured Liver Birds nesting on columns. There's also a 7ft high relief called Speed: the Modern Mercury (wearing a racing helmet and goggles) plus four more figures representing Civil Engineering, Construction, Architecture and Decoration and holding, respectively, a cross-section of a tunnel, model of trabeation (beams used in construction), Ionic capital and Assyrian capital with back-to-back crouching bulls.

Then as now, the building provides a fabulous contrast to the dominant Victorian gothic and neo-classical architecture of Liverpool. And to think its sole function is to pump used air out of the Mersey Tunnel.

(K)night...

And Day

Pier Head

Lusitania propeller

■ One of four 23-ton propellers from the Cunard liner Lusitania, which was torpedoed by a German U-Boat off southern Ireland in May 1915 while returning to Liverpool from New York. One of the largest and most luxurious ships afloat, the Lusitania left the Mersey on her maiden voyage to America in 1907, the propellers rotating at three times a second and driving the ship across the Atlantic at over 26 knots (30mph). Her sinking caused the loss of 1,201 lives and precipitated the USA's entry into the First World War.

Bird? Plane? No, Albert Duck

Albert Dock

■ You've left the Museum of Liverpool Life and are now approaching the largest group of Grade I listed buildings in England – one of the earliest enclosed docks in the world and something akin to a waterfront castle. A triumph of function and design, they were conceived in 1846 by Jesse Hartley (the city's Dock Engineer) and consist of five formidable warehouses – check out the sheer bulk of their sandstone and granite slabs – each five storeys high with a combined capacity of 250,000 tons. They were almost demolished in the early 1980s to make way for a car park and university premises. Today the whole area is a conservation site embracing Tate Liverpool, the Maritime Museum, bars and restaurants, shops and flats, the Canning and Salthouse Docks, a pumping station, swing bridges, watchmen's huts and pier master's house. And what about those vistas…

Walk this way 056

2. Business District

■ Wander up James Street or Water Street from the Pier Head and the whiff of commerce hits you straightaway. The architecture of the Business District is overwhelmingly Victorian – with the occasional, glorious Art Deco intrusion – and a reaction to the growth of Liverpool's docks in preceding decades, with rows of elegant premises along the city's seven original streets (Dale, Water, Tithebarn, Chapel, Old Hall, High and Castle). Many of these buildings were once banks or exchanges for every form of commodity from cotton to corn to fruit, and the whole district is rich in symbolism and steeped in history – if you know just where to look.

Walk this way

2. Business District

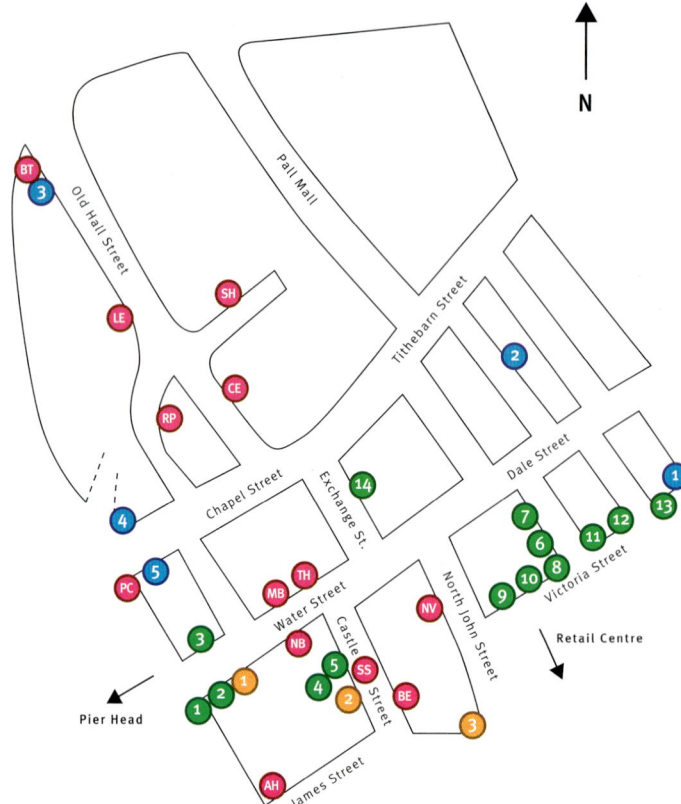

The attractions...
- BT Beetham Tower
- LE Liverpool Daily Post & Echo
- SH Stanley Hall
- CE Cotton Exchange
- RP Rumford Place
- PC Parish Church
- MB Martins Bank
- TH Town Hall
- NB National Bank
- AH Albion House
- BE Bank of England
- NV North John Street Ventilation Tower
- SS Sanctuary Stone

The hotels...
1. Sir Thomas Hotel
2. Travel Inn
3. Radisson SAS
4. Thistle
5. Racquet Club

Is there an Echo in here?

City Exchange

■ Home to the Liverpool Daily Post & Echo, the city's morning and evening newspapers, and one of the best modern frontages in Liverpool. The light and spacious, multi-level atrium provides enhanced access from the street and stages everything from photographic exhibitions to private parties and trade fairs under its stunning tubular canopy.

Walk this way   058

Get the bales in

Cotton Exchange

■ The ornate Edwardian façade may have gone, but this place is steeped in history. It's the headquarters of the Liverpool Cotton Association, opened in 1906 by the Prince and Princess of Wales (their signatures are on the opening page of the priceless visitor's book). Back then, 5million bales of raw cotton were imported to Liverpool every year. Today, over 60 per cent of the world's cotton is still traded under LCA rules. Outside the Exchange is an alleorical statue of the River Mersey, and in the courtyard are two statues of Navigation and Commerce, the only survivors of eight that once stood high up on the roof.

There's a lift, luckily

Beetham Tower

■ The latest addition to the waterfront skyline. At 30 storeys it's the tallest new residential building in England's North West, and all 120 apartments were snapped up within three weeks. Its landscaped gardens, though, come free of charge and feature walls with illuminated portholes portraying the faces of contemporary Liverpudlians. That's modern art, that is.

The bars and restaurants...

1. Simply Heathcotes
2. Platinum Lounge
3. Newz Bar
4. Slaughterhouse
5. Franco's
6. Algarve
7. Casa Italia
8. Superstar Boudoir
9. Metro
10. Pacific Bar & Grill
11. Living Room
12. Don Pepe
13. Sultan's Palace
14. Anderson's

The shops...

1. Circa 1900
2. Bang & Olufsen
3. Boodle & Dunthorne

Where Bulloch broke the Union blockade

It happened here...

■ Rumford Place is the little corner of Liverpool that's forever America. The Star Spangled Banner recalls its former incarnation, at the outbreak of the US Civil War 140 years ago, as the premises of Charleston cotton merchants, John Fraser and Co. With two-thirds of American cotton coming through Liverpool they were also the European bankers for the Confederacy.

When the Union threw a blockade around Confederate ports in 1861, Captain James Bulloch was sent secretly from Georgia to England with $1milion to build ships that would break the siege. He stayed at Rumford Place and, with the aid of fellow agent Isidor Straus (an American immigrant originally from Georgia in the Caucasus), financed the construction of 35 'raiders' – most notoriously the Alabama that destroyed or captured over 60 Union vessels.

The last surrender of the war was made on 6 November 1865 by his final ship, the Shenandoah, on the Mersey – but to the British government rather than the Union. Bulloch was denied amnesty by the US and remained in Liverpool for the rest of his life. He died in 1901 and was buried at Toxteth Cemetery. Straus was allowed to return home, eventually buying Macy's department store in New York and becoming one of the world's richest men. He died on the Titanic in 1912 and was buried at Woodlawn Cemetery in the Bronx.

Rumford Place had another visitor in 1958. By then it was home to the Mercantile Marine Service Association, which was approached by a retired mariner trying to clear his name upon the release of the movie A Night To Remember. Stanley Lord had been captain of the Californian, the ship bound for Boston from Liverpool that reportedly ignored the Titanic's distress signals. He died four years later, aged 84, at his home in Wallasey on the Wirral.

Albion House

■ A beautiful building on the corner of the Strand and James Street, with alternating bands of red brick and Portland Stone (the architect Richard Shaw also designed New Scotland Yard in London). It was built for the Oceanic Steam Navigation Company, or White Star Line, and it was here that many of the crew of the Titanic were enlisted. It was here, too, that their relatives converged, desperate for news when the ship sank in April 1912.

Walk this way 060

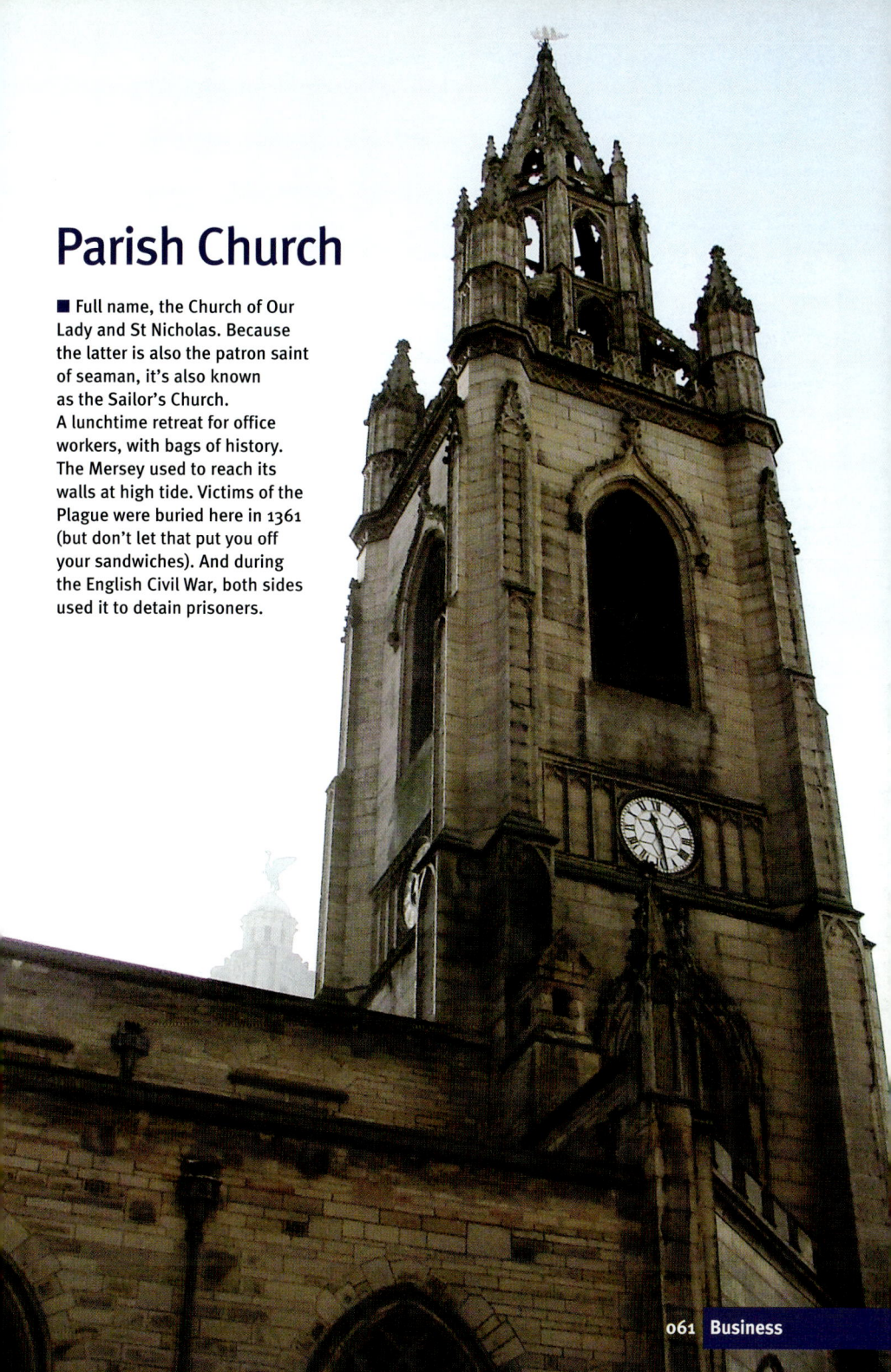

Parish Church

■ Full name, the Church of Our Lady and St Nicholas. Because the latter is also the patron saint of seaman, it's also known as the Sailor's Church. A lunchtime retreat for office workers, with bags of history. The Mersey used to reach its walls at high tide. Victims of the Plague were buried here in 1361 (but don't let that put you off your sandwiches). And during the English Civil War, both sides used it to detain prisoners.

Martins Bank Building

■ A truly great Liverpool building, it's actually one of the finest realisations of early American commercial architecture in the UK. Designed for the old Martins Bank in 1932 by Herbert Rowse (the genius behind the India Building, Philharmonic Hall and George's Dock Building), its exterior is decorated with maritime motifs and Liver Birds topped by grasshoppers – a reference to the name of the Liverpool tavern where a moneylender practised the city's first banking system in the late 16th century.
The eighth-floor boardroom is just as fabulous, with a walnut ceiling swimming in mermaids, dolphins, seahorses and starfish. During the Second World War the building stored Britain's gold bullion reserves for shipment to Canada should the country be invaded, and it's been home to Barclays since 1969.

Building of interest in more ways than one

Bank of England Building

■ Grade I listed and designed by Charles Cockerill, who also finished St George's Hall after the untimely death of Harvey Lonsdale Elmes (see Cultural Quarter). Striking in appearance and classically Greek in detail, it looks bigger than it is – which is exactly what the architect intended.

All in the detail: balcony, Martins Bank Building

063 **Business**

No place like dome

Town Hall

■ The third Town Hall to stand on this site, and one of Liverpool's Georgian gems. Queen Victoria, Mark Twain, the Beatles and the city's football teams have graced its balcony, while Minerva, Roman goddess of wisdom, presides from the dome above. At the rear, looking onto Exchange Flags (the city's original cotton exchange), are statues of the four seasons which came from the Irish Houses of Parliament. Home to the Lord Mayor, a grand staircase, portraits of past royalty, a banqueting room, two ballrooms and three crystal chandeliers (72 gas burners each). Grade I listed.

Sanctuary Stone

■ Embedded in the road surface outside the NatWest Bank on Castle Street (watch the traffic), this ancient stone marks the boundary of the old Liverpool Fairs held on 25 July and 11 November each year, when debtors were allowed to conduct lawful business free from arrest.

Why did they do it in the road?

Walk this way 064

3. Shopping Centre

■ The hub of Liverpool's six walking zones may be retail-based, but it has just as much to offer in terms of the arts, heritage and architecture. Woolworth's, for example, opened its first British store on Church Street in 1909. On the site next door, Harrods seriously considered setting up shop 15 years later, actually commissioning a design from the day's leading architects. And in how many other shopping centres around the UK would you find a Big Willie stuck to the outside of a major department store? Look out, too, for the birthplace of a popular 60s musical act called The Beatles. Wonder whatever became of them...

3. Shopping Centre

The attractions...
- **OB** Observatory
- **CC** Conservation Centre
- **WS** Williamson Square
- **PT** Playhouse Theatre
- **SB** St. John's Beacon
- **NT** Neptune Theatre
- **AT** Athenaeum
- **BC** Bluecoat Chambers
- **WC** PCT Walk-in Centre

The hotels...
1. Marriot City
2. Holiday Inn
3. Moat House

The bars and restaurants...
1. Orchid Spring
2. Puccino's
3. Grapes
4. Dr. Duncan's
5. Queen Square (Honey Harmony, Ask, La Tasca etc)

Vivienne Westwood — 11

■ Launched by the lady herself in autumn 2003, Liverpool's first dedicated designer's boutique opens up onto Mathew Street from Cavern Walks (whose terracotta decoration, incidentally, was designed by Cynthia Lennon). It's worth a visit for the store's fabulous interior alone – there's a stunning chandelier, giant fragrance bottles, glittering cabinets and HRH's portrait on the wall. And have clothes ever looked so sexy on their hangers?

Walk this way 066

It happened here...

■ Music. Liverpool. Mathew Street. This is history, folks, the real deal. Ready? From the North John Street entrance, the first statue is a life-size Lennon dressed in leather jacket over roll-neck sweater and jeans, leaning against a doorway (from the cover of his 1975 album Rock 'n' Roll). Next to him is the Wall of Fame, unveiled in 1997 to celebrate the 40th anniversary of the opening of the Cavern Club, the old site of which is just across the road (The Rolling Stones, The Who, Chuck Berry, Rod Stewart and Stevie Wonder also played here). The Wall features the name of every one of Liverpool's 54 No1 chart hits since 1952 (it's in the Guinness Book of Records as the World Capital of Pop). Nearby, Four Lads Who Shook the World, a sculpture by Arthur Dooley of 'Mother Liverpool' holding Paul, George and Ringo, with John wearing a halo to the right. Inside Cavern Walks is John Doubleday's more conventional Beatles statue, and further down the street, above The Beatles Shop, is a bronze bust of the band entitled From Us To You, by David Hughes.

The shops...

1. Church Steet (BHS, Gap, Boots, JJB Sports, Marks & Spencer, John Lewis, Open, Littlewoods, Dorothy Perkins, Burtons, Top Shop, HMV, Next, WH Smith etc)
2. Quiggins Centre
3. Sevenoaks Sound & Vision
4. Wade Smith
5. Reiss
6. Designer City
7. Liverpool FC Superstore
8. St John's Centre
9. Clayton Square
10. Cavern Walks
11. Vivienne Westwood

Eleanor Rigby

■ Bronze sculpture dedicated to 'All the Lonely People' and presented to the city of Liverpool in 1982. Her creator Tommy Steele placed a children's comic, page from the Bible, four-leaf clover, pair of football boots and four love sonnets inside the figure, so she'd "be full of magical properties." Eleanor Rigby was a name on a headstone in a church cemetery in Woolton (south Liverpool) where John and Paul first met.

Wearing the face that she keeps in a jar by the door

067 **Shopping**

Church Street

■ Some fine classical buildings on the city's main shopping artery. Compton House, now home to Marks and Spencer, was originally a draper's store then a hotel (you can just make out the name in the top right corner of the old picture). It was designed in 1867 by Gerald de Courcy Fraser, who was also the architect for the adjacent John Lewis building on Basnett Street constructed just after the First World War. Yes, that really is a Mark I tank, or 'Big Willie', protruding from the wall.

Bluecoat Chambers

■ At the end of Church Alley is the city-centre's oldest building and arguably its most elegant. It was built by a sea captain and an inscription on the outside reads: 'Dedicated to the promotion of Christian charity and the training of poor boys in the principles of the Anglican Church. Founded this year of salvation 1717'. Now home to the Bluecoat Arts and Display Centres, with a tree-lined courtyard and new wing housing a gallery and performance space under construction.

The Great Escape

■ One of Liverpool's most intriguing landmarks, weighing over three tons and created by Edward Cronshaw, whose figurative work shows Mexican and Romanesque influences and is a reaction against 'dimensional and decorative' modern sculpture. A horse, a man and a popular rendezvous for shoppers and pigeons.

Athenaeum

■ On Church Alley, before the Bluecoat, is the only Liverpool 'newsroom' still in existence – a private club founded in 1797 as 'a meeting place where ideas and information could be exchanged in pleasant surroundings'. With a library, dining room and lounge bar, today it's hired for functions and parties.

St John's Beacon

■ Towering over the cityscape at 450ft high, this was once a restaurant and is now the HQ of Radio City. Near its base is the St John's Shopping Centre on the site of the old St John's Market, itself a beautiful building with 130 arched window-bays that was captured for posterity by watercolour artist Samuel Austin in 1827. In the painting below (on display at the Lady Lever Gallery on the Wirral) are two black figures – a page and woman worker – suggesting that arrivals from Africa and the Americas had become a relatively integrated part of Liverpool life by the early 19th Century.

Williamson Square

■ The arching water-jet fountain is a more recent addition to this popular public space between Church Street and Queen Square that accommodates the legendary Playhouse Theatre (the most recent Liverpool building to be listed – more specifically its glazed and cantilevered complex of foyers, bars and restaurants, in 1975 and 1999 respectively). Charles Dickens once performed as an actor here, in its earlier incarnation as the Theatre Royal.

Liverpool Resurgent

■ Striding forward on the prow of a ship jutting over the entrance to Lewis's department store on Ranelagh Street (opposite the Adelphi Hotel) and known locally as Dickie Lewis for fairly self-evident reasons. He was created in 1954 by Jacob Epstein (born in New York, studied with Rodin in Paris) to symbolise the city's indomitability after 68 air raids during the Second World War.

Paradise found...

■ Less than two centuries ago Liverpool's south docklands, and particularly the area around Paradise Street, were 'in depravity not to be matched by anything this side of the pit that is bottomless', according to novelist Herman Melville, who arrived here as a cabin boy from New York in 1839. Today Paradise Street is the epicentre of the biggest retail development in Europe – a £750million scheme over 43 acres, extending into Church Street and Canning Place (opposite the Albert Dock) and reaching as far as Rope Walks. The man in charge is the Duke of Westminster, the richest man in Britain. He's promising 20 modern, world-class buildings that will house shops, hotels, apartments, offices and leisure facilities, and there'll be a new elevated public space at Chavasse Park. Scheduled for completion in 2007, on the occasion of Liverpool's 800th birthday.

Shopping

the Walker
national gallery of the North

And when did you last see...

William Brown Street, Liverpool.
0151 478 4199
www.thewalker.org.uk

CONSERVATION CENTRE

Revealing objects
Past
Present
Future...

WHITECHAPEL
LIVERPOOL
0151 478 4999
www.conservationcentre.org.uk

Liverpool Museum

William Brown Street, Liverpool.
0151 478 4393
www.liverpoolmuseum.org.uk

LIFELINES
A STORY OF MERCHANT SHIPS AND SEAFARERS

MERSEYSIDE MARITIME MUSEUM
ALBERT DOCK, LIVERPOOL
0151 478 4499
www.merseysidemaritimemuseum.org.uk

INCORPORATING
HM CUSTOMS & EXCISE NATIONAL MUSEUM
www.customsandexcisemuseum.org.uk

Museum of Liverpool Life

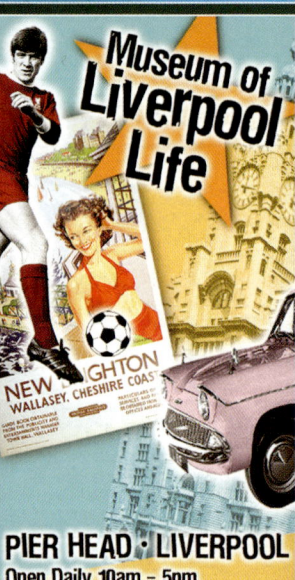

PIER HEAD · LIVERPOOL
Open Daily 10am – 5pm
www.museumofliverpoollife.org.uk
Tel 0151 478 4080

LADY LEVER ART GALLERY

PORT SUNLIGHT, WIRRAL
0151 478 4136
www.ladyleverartgallery.org.uk

Why not also visit
SUDLEY HOUSE
MOSSLEY HILL
0151 724 3245
www.sudleyhouse.org.uk

FREE ENTRY   NATIONAL MUSEUMS LIVERPOOL

4. Cultural Quarter

■ Welcome to what the recently-published Pevsner architectural guide to Liverpool hails as 'a piece of romantic classical urban scenery [with] no equal in England'. William Brown Street was named after an Irish cotton trader who emigrated to America in 1800 then settled in Liverpool 12 years later, financing the construction of the city's first museum and library. Already, St George's Hall had been opened and the quarter was earmarked as a manifestation of Liverpool's civic pride, with the buildings along Lime Street designed to reflect this grandeur, and today it's a Conservation Area. The nearby Royal Alexandra Theatre & Opera House was erected in 1866 and replaced by the Empire Theatre (we insist you take in the brilliant view from the café-bar) in 1925. The seven-storey North Western Hotel (now providing student accommodation) was designed in 1871 by Alfred Waterhouse – the same architect behind London's Natural History Museum. And the train station, at one end of the world's first true public railway, boasted the world's first iron shed with the world's largest arched span (200ft). Breathtaking stuff, we think you'll agree.

Walk this way

4. Cultural Quarter

The attractions...

- **LM** Liverpool Museum
- **CL** Central Library
- **WG** Walker Art Gallery
- **CS** County Sessions House
- **WC** Wellington's Column & Steble Fountain
- **QT** Queensway Tunnel
- **SG** St George's Hall
- **SJ** St John's Gardens
- **ET** Empire Theatre
- **CA** Carling Academy
- **LS** Lime Street Station

The hotels...

- **1** Gladstone
- **2** Travelodge

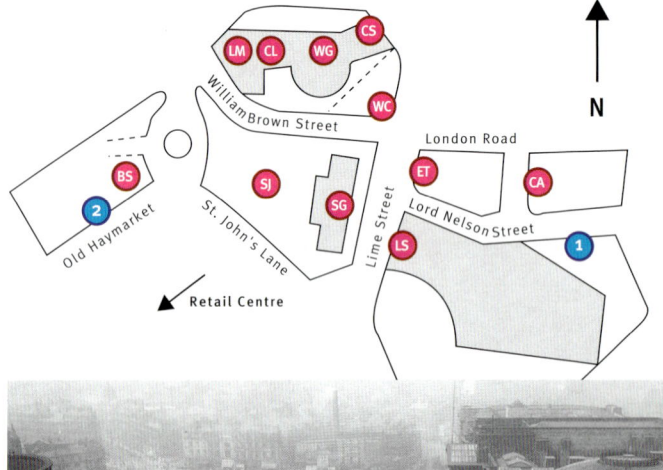

William Brown Street from Wellington's Column in 1913

It happened here...

■ On 18 July 1934, King George V and Queen Mary officially opened Queensway, designed by Herbert Rowse as the longest underwater road tunnel in the world and a deliberately modernist contrast to the neo-classical style of the Cultural Quarter's grand buildings. Queensway even has its own coat of arms. Between two giant winged bulls ('symbolic of swift and heavy traffic') stand Apollo and Pluto, the gods of light and darkness. The shield between them contains a Liver Bird and two stars below two lions holding a wheel. The motto underneath is Ripae Ulterioris Amore. It's from Virgil's Aeneid and means, 'In longing for the further bank'.

Liverpool Museum

■ The first of the William Brown Street buildings, constructed in 1860 in the same Greco-Roman style of St George's Hall, which had stood for 15 years.

An annexe, originally housing a Technical School, was added in 1901. Above its entrance is a symbolic sculpture of Liverpool holding a globe and sceptre, flanked by Commerce and Industry. Note the seahorses on the bronze lamp standards (right) by the corner of Byrom Street, designed by Frederick Pomeroy. Believe it or not, he went on to design the first Mr Universe statuette in America.

Central Library

■ Built in conjunction with the Museum, this was the first original free library in the country. Today it has 600,000 visitors every year. The drum-shaped Picton Reading Room, following the curve in the street and modelled on the British Museum Reading Room, was added in 1879 and became the first building in the city to have electric lighting. By 2008, Central Library will be reinvented as a World Discovery Centre connected to the Museum and Walker by an internal walkway, with its 90million archives on Liverpool's history digitised to create an online genealogy service linked to Ellis Island Visitor Centre in New York.

The Walker

■ The first major public art gallery outside London, styled as a Roman temple and named after the local brewer who paid for its construction in 1870. The seated statues of Michelangelo (left) and Raphael, representing sculpture and painting, were carved by John Warrington Wood in Italy. The allegorical Liverpool on the roof is a copy of his original, now in the Conservation Centre (see page 166).

County Sessions House

■ The last of the set, opened in 1884 and featuring four pairs of Corinthian columns and the Lancashire coat of arms on its pediment. There's a fine Italian Renaissance staircase inside, but you'll have to wait till the next Heritage Open Day (every September) to see it.

Steble Fountain

■ Unveiled in 1879 as a gift to the city from its mayor, RF Steble. The cast-iron figures around the base are Neptune, Amphitrite (his wife), Acis (a river deity) and Galatea (sea nymph). It's a copy of an original designed by French artist Paul Lienard for the Paris World Fair of 1855. There's another version called the Brewer Fountain outside Massachusetts State House in Boston (right) as well as replicas in Lyons, Bordeaux, Geneva and Cairo.

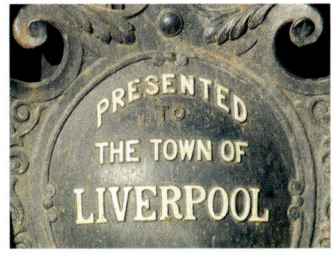

St George's Hall

■ The royal favourite. On a tour of Liverpool in 1851, Queen Victoria said it was "worthy of ancient Athens, the architecture is so simple and magnificent." More recently Prince Charles called it "one of the greatest public buildings of the last 200 years which sits in the centre of one of Europe's finest cities." Who are we to argue?

This 490ft long, neo-classical masterpiece was designed by 23-year-old Harvey Lonsdale Elmes, who died a decade later from consumption. It has a 7,737-pipe organ, an exquisite sunken floor covered with blue and brown Minton tiles, and stained-glass windows at either end depicting Liverpool's coat of arms and St George and the Dragon.

Above all, it's an emphatic declaration of the city's status as the second city of the British Empire. On the six pairs of bronze doors inside are the letters SPQL, an adaptation of the motto of Rome and meaning 'to the Senate and the People of Liverpool'. Outside, a pride of four lions, each 14ft long, stand guard while the building undergoes an £18m refurbishment.

Walk this way 080

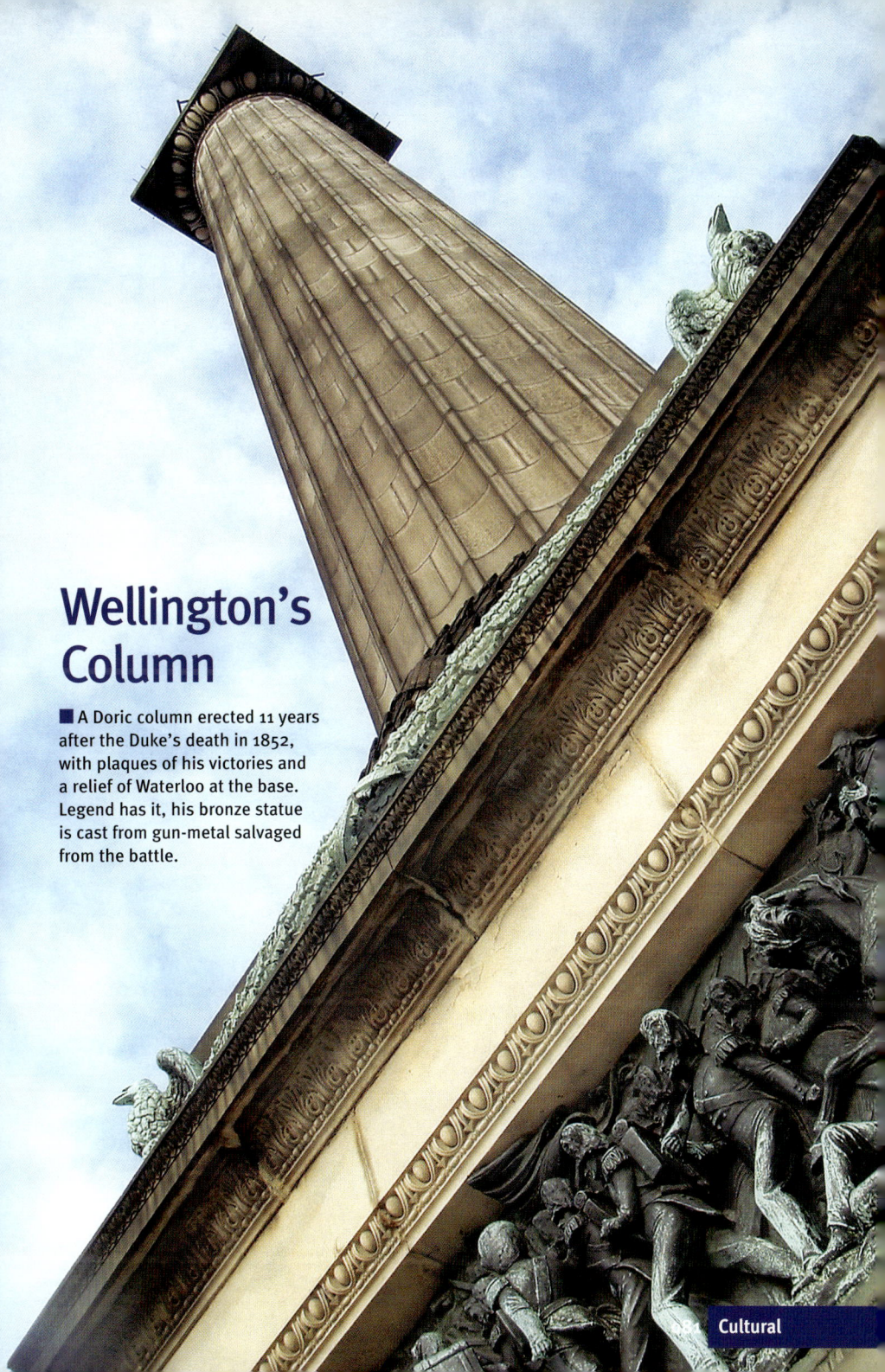

Wellington's Column

■ A Doric column erected 11 years after the Duke's death in 1852, with plaques of his victories and a relief of Waterloo at the base. Legend has it, his bronze statue is cast from gun-metal salvaged from the battle.

Cultural

St John's Gardens

■ A sloping, tranquil terrace, opened in 1904 on the grounds of a former church from which it takes its name. There are several monuments to Liverpool's great and good (among them William Gladstone) and many of the city's 30 war memorials are here (including one to 357 members of the King's Liverpool Regiment lost in Afghanistan, Burma and South Africa). More recently a memorial was unveiled to commemorate the 60th anniversary of D-Day.

5. Rope Walks

■ If it feels like you're in an urban village, it's because you are. A 24/7 tumult of activity, this historic area really was a ropery at the turn of the 19th Century, supplying the sailing ships of the age. Its vibe today comes from the feeling of flux when you wander up Bold Street, through the crowds and multi-lingual chatter, past the buskers, specialist stores and charismatic cafés and delis with their late Georgian and mock Florentine facades on a thoroughfare once compared with London's Bond Street, and hang a right through a warren of hard hats, drills and cranes to the artist studios of Duke Street and the beginning of Chinatown. It's a noisy, anarchic work in process, criss-crossed with squares, gardens and walkways, and blessed with 90 listed buildings and an embarrassment of bars and clubs.

5. Rope Walks

The attractions...
- **CS** Campbell Square
- **WS** Wolstenholme Square
- **CO** Concert Square
- **FA** FACT Centre
- **EU** East Village
- **CA** Chinese Arch

The shops...
1. Bold Street (Karen Millen, Drome, Zen, Utility, Lotus Room)
2. Liverpool Palace

The bars and restaurants...
1. Prohibition
2. Velvet Lounge
3. Soul Café
4. Tea Factory
5. Society
6. Jacaranda
7. 3345
8. Hemingways
9. Christakis/ St Petersburg

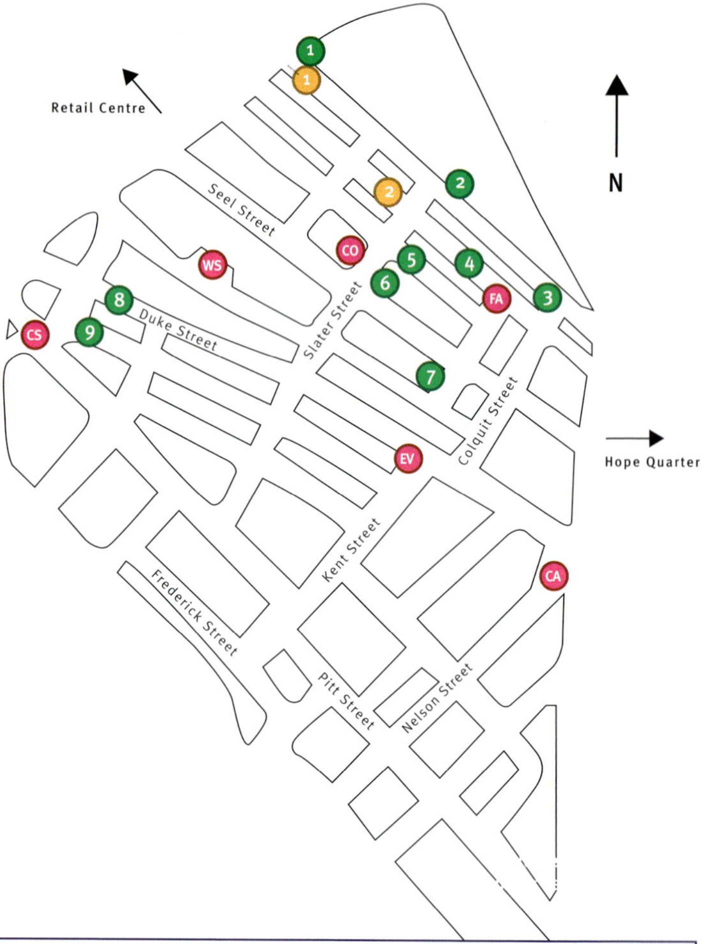

It happened here...

■ The origins of Europe's oldest Chinatown lie in the Blue Funnel Line's direct trade routes between Liverpool and China, which commenced in 1865. Six years later there were over 200 Chinese people living here, and 1886 saw the first Chinese laundry in the city. Here you'll also find the country's first Chinese pub, The Nook. Nelson Street remains the hub – walk down it today and you'll still hear mah jong being played upstairs. The 15-metre Chinese Arch, a gift from sister-city Shanghai, is a blaze of gold, red, green and yellow adorned with 200 dragons. It marks a conduit down to the river according to the principles of feng shui.

Walk this way 084

The Lyceum

- A grand old building in the Greek Revival style (those six columns are just being Ionic), over 200 years old and at the bottom of Bold Street. Designed by Thomas Harrison, in its heyday it was the joint premises of a gentlemen's club and one of the oldest circulating libraries in the country, then the Post Office and now Prohibition bar. Above the windows are reliefs of Navigation, The Arts (represented by Apollo) and Commerce, and inside are friezes adapted from the Parthenon and a domed gallery with a skylight.

Back to work...

- Between Bold Street and Duke Street lies one of the largest concentration of historic warehouses in the country – some of which still have the 'cat heads' used to hoist goods – while the shorter, narrower streets between them are crammed with former yards, works, kilns and breweries. Many are being converted to new uses with names that reflect their old role (Paper Mill, Cinammon Building, Vanilla Factory etc). The grand total in development costs is £150million.

It happened here, too...

Wolstenholme Square

- Historically the first enclosed garden in Liverpool and home to Tate's tobacco and snuff firm before it housed the world-famous Cream nightclub. Now occupied by the arching tentacles of Penelope, a public sculpture unveiled in summer 2004 (see page 176).

085 Rope Walks

East Village

■ A large, striking complex of apartments with a Manhattan theme (Hudson Gardens, Liberty Village etc) and balconies overlooking landscaped gardens. Earmarked to be Liverpool's premier restaurant quarter, with Japanese sushi bar Sapporo Teppanyaki already dishing out the yellow-fin tuna and pickled ginger, and more eateries planned around a central courtyard with fountains set flush in the paving. A flagship of urban living in Liverpool.

"And then Chris Martin turns to me and says..."

Parr Street Studios

■ Three studios, award-winning producers and the biggest residential recording complex outside London. Among the musicians who've worked here: Coldplay, Gomez, The Spice Girls, Atomic Kitten, Elbow, Badly Drawn Boy, Embrace, Sophie Ellis-Bextor, Super Furry Animals, Starsailor, Stereophonics, The Doves and Mansun. Nice café-bar and restaurant, too.

Duke's Terrace

■ Home to some of Liverpool's wealthiest and most fashionable merchants 140 years ago, this Grade II listed terrace on Upper Duke Street has been refurbished as four buildings set around a courtyard, with interiors based on the original 19th Century layout.

Tea Factory

■ Formerly the premises of Mantunna, it's now a £10million, mixed-use scheme with Bluu Bar and the Tea Factory Bar & Kitchen based at ground-level and offices and plush penthouses on top. There's also gallery and exhibition space at CUBE (Centre for the Understanding of the Built Environment) and the northern offices of RIBA (Royal Institute of British Architects) next door. All linked by a new square to St Peter's on Fleet Street, the city's oldest church (founded in 1788 as a Benedictine mission).

FACT

■ Due east from the Tea Factory, the Foundation for Arts and Creative Technologies is the city's first purpose-built arts centre for more than 60 years, and very different in character to the surrounding red-brick warehouses. The emphasis is upon transparency and public access, with cantilevered stairs inside and glazed facades looking out across the Liverpool cityscape. Throughout the building, the calm colours of natural materials provide a suitable backdrop for the art on display.

Walk this way   088

6. Hope Quarter

■ On the brow of the big city sits a special place – a world of handsome Georgian properties, cobbled alleyways, awesome cathedrals and delightful pubs and restaurants. This was the address of Liverpool's most affluent citizens in the 19th Century, and today it's still a leafy retreat from the city-centre as well as a hotbed of arts, culture and academia, blending seamlessly into the main University campus. Take in the great views down to the Pier Head, and take time to explore the Hope Quarter's bucolic nooks and crannies. There is sweet music here...

Walk this way

6. Hope Quarter

The attractions...

- **GC** Grand Central Hall
- **SA** St Andrew's Church
- **MC** Metropolitan Cathedral
- **ET** Everyman Theatre
- **PH** Philharmonic Hall
- **PN** St Philip Neri/ Spanish Garden
- **AC** Anglican Cathedral
- **SJ** St James Cemetery
- **LP** LIPA
- **CH** Chambre-Hardman House
- **UT** Unity Theatre
- **AP** Arthur Clough Plaque
- **GB** Gladstone's Birthplace
- **SL** St Luke's Church

Walk this way 090

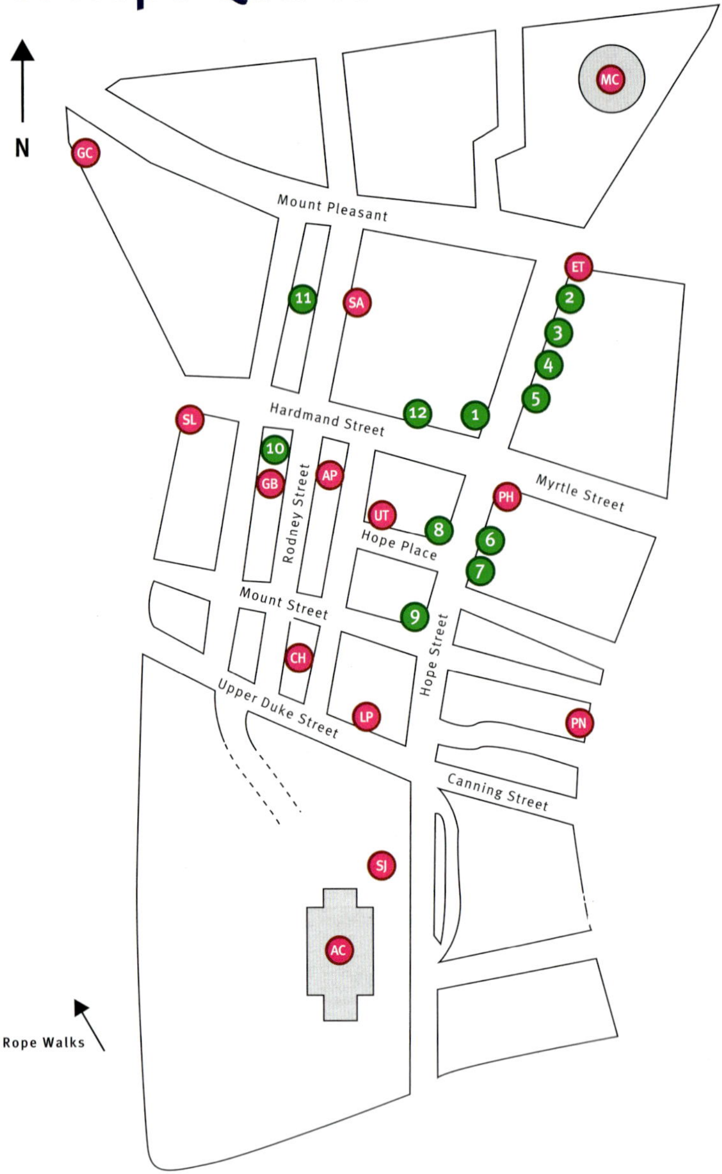

Grand Central Auditorium

■ On Renshaw Street so not technically Hope Quarter, but too grand to miss out. This was the original meeting-place of Liverpool's Unitarians, who had their roots in the non-conformist movement of the 17th Century (like Islam and Judaism believing God was one and Jesus a prophet to be followed rather than worshipped). They were a powerful, free-thinking influence in the city, counting philanthropist and abolitionist William Roscoe among their congregation (he's buried in the adjacent gardens named after him). In 1899 they moved their church to Ullet Road (see page 174).

The bars and restaurants...

- ① Philharmonic Hotel
- ② Everyman Bistro
- ③ Casa
- ④ El Macho
- ⑤ Other Place
- ⑥ Lower Place
- ⑦ Ego
- ⑧ London Carriage Works
- ⑨ 60 Hope Street
- ⑩ Valparaiso
- ⑪ Puschka
- ⑫ Magnet

St Luke's Church

■ Or the 'Bombed-out Church' as locals call it. Dominating the top of Bold Street, on the corner of Berry Street and Leece Street, it was completed in 1831 but damaged during the Second World War and now stands as a memorial to peace and place of tranquillity. There's a monument to Irish emigrants and the Great Famine near the entrance gates on Leece Street.

Philharmonic Hotel

■ Not so much a public house as a work of genius. Built in 1900 to the designs of Royal Liver Building architect Walter Aubrey Thomas (with a little help from the University's School of Art), it features caryatids (sculptured female figures serving as pillars), plaster friezes, copper panels, stained glass and splendid decoration throughout. Much of the joinery work was carried out by ship's carpenters used to working on the interiors of transatlantic liner. A public bar, grande lounge and snugs called Brahms and Liszt.

St Andrew's Church

■ The pyramid tomb in the Grade II listed graveyard of this Rodney Street church is thought to hold the body of railway engineer and infamous poker player William Mackenzie, sitting at a table holding a Royal Flush. According to legend, he sold his soul to the devil and believed that being laid to rest above ground would save him from damnation. Spooky.

Rodney Street

■ These days the Georgian terraces of Liverpool's Harley Street are home to physiotherapists, chiropodists, acupuncturists and dental surgeons. But they're also an historical Who's Who of the city. Ready for this? James Maury, the first US Consul in Liverpool, lived at no4 from 1790 to 1829. Nos9, 11, 34 and 62 were the respective birthplaces of poet Arthur Clough (friend of Longfellow and Thackeray), naval officer and author Nicholas Monsarrat (The Cruel Sea), Henry Booth (founder of the Liverpool & Manchester Railway) and William Gladstone (four times Prime Minister). Radiology pioneer C Thurston Holland worked at no43. William Duncan, Liverpool's first Medical Officer of Health, lived at no54. And Lytton Strachey, biographer and Bloomsbury Group confidante of Virginia Wolf, once occupied no80.

Chambre-Hardman House

■ At 59 Rodney Street, the time-capsule home and studio of photographer Edward Chambre-Hardman has been converted into an interactive museum by the National Trust with Heritage Lottery funding, and was opened to the public in 2004 following a preview exhibition at Central Library (called E Chambre-Hardman: Behind the Lens). He was born in Dublin and moved to Liverpool in the early 1920s, capturing liners sailing in and out of the port, the construction of the aircraft-carrier Ark Royal and superstars like Ivor Novello, Robert Donat and Margot Fonteyn at the Playhouse (for whom he was the official photographer). Twenty of his best-known works, along with the tools of his trade (including camera and 150,000 prints, negatives and glass plates), are now displayed in this restored 1940s interior.

Philharmonic Hall

■ It's been called 'frozen music' and it's that man Herbert Rowse again – this time fusing modernist style with acoustic data to design another landmark building (after the original hall's fire in 1933). He described it as "shaped like a megaphone with the orchestra at the narrow end." Inside, there are etched-glass decorations, gilded reliefs of Apollo and a memorial to the musicians of the Titanic. Rowse's initials, it's claimed, are woven into the sumptuous carpets.

It happened here...

■ In 1836 Charles Dickens gave a speech at the Mechanics Institute (now LIPA) in the first of 19 visits to Liverpool. He usually stayed at the Adelphi Hotel, sailed twice from the city to America, fell in love with a girl from Breck Road in Anfield, walked New Brighton's sands and gave public readings of his books at the Philharmonic Hall and St George's Hall (he once called Liverpool "the Copperfield stronghold"). Off Park Road, just south of the city-centre, is a row of streets called Pickwick, Dombey and Dorrit, crossed by Dickens Street.

Metropolitan Cathedral

■ 'Paddy's Wigwam' and one of the sights that makes Liverpool, so Liverpool. Frederick Gibberd's epitome of 1960s monumental concrete design was completed in 1967 and boasts the world's largest stained-glass window in its Lantern Tower, which itself weighs 2,000 tons. A new approach and ramp have been added to the main entrance, which has panels depicting the winged emblems of the Evangelists – the man of Matthew, lion of Mark, ox of Luke and eagle of John.

Anglican Cathedral

■ You can't see Bede, David, Paul, Chad, Gilbert, Guthlac, Michael, Nicholas, Martin, Peter, Oswald, James and Emmanuel. But boy, can you can hear them. The 13 mighty bells – Emmanuel alone weighs four tons – of this colossal Cathedral possess the heaviest and highest ringing peal in the world. Designed by Giles Gilbert Scott, a 23-year-old Roman Catholic, the Anglican was 100 years old on 19 July 2004 (the main image shows the work completed by 1936). And at 101,000sq ft – almost twice the size of St Paul's in London – it's the fifth largest cathedral in the world (behind St Peter's in Rome, St John in New York, Nativity of Mary in Milan and Mary of the Chair in Seville). Near the entrance is John Foster's delightful and much earlier Oratory, a miniature Greek temple.

Kitty Wilkinson, died 1860, 'unwearied nurse of the sick'

Capt Elisha Halsey of Charleston, lost in the Bay of Biscay

St James Cemetery

■ In the shadow of the Anglican Cathedral is the most romantic cemetery in England, declared full in 1936 after almost 58,000 internments. Originally a vast quarry accessed via ramps and subterranean walkways, it has an ancient spring and graffiti dating back to 1727 (see page 89) carved into the sandstone walls. Sons and daughters of Kentucky, South Carolina, New York, New Jersey, Massachusetts and Pennsylvania are all buried here, and there are countless memorials to those that perished at sea.

Canning Street

■ Feel like you've just stepped back in time? This street, together with Percy Street, Huskisson Street, Falkner Square and Gambier Terrace, comprises a conservation area of supremely elegant late Georgian and Victorian housing with columned porches and grand balconies. Once home to Liverpool's gentry, it has a much younger population these days and is regularly commandeered by camera crews for period dramas (David Copperfield, Sherlock Holmes, Forsyte Saga etc).

El Jardin della Nuestra Senora

Spanish Garden

■ In the grounds of St Philip Neri's Church on Catharine Street, and a labour of love for its old reverend in the early 1950s. He paid a visit to the rooftop garden at Barkers department store on London's Kensington High Street and decided to create his own paradise on the Blitz-scarred land adjacent to his church. Passion flowers, marble columns, a water nymph and (allegedly) a fragment of a pillar from Gladstone's old address on Rodney Street.

University of Liverpool

■ The original red-brick university, founded in 1881 and now one of the leading research universities. It's spawned eight Nobel Laureates, including Sir James Chadwick for discovery of the neutron in 1936. The coat of arms has an open book with the motto Fiat Lux, meaning 'Let There Be Light', between three silver Liver Birds that represent Liverpool as a seaport, seat of a bishopric and founder of University College.

Walk this way 100

World in one city

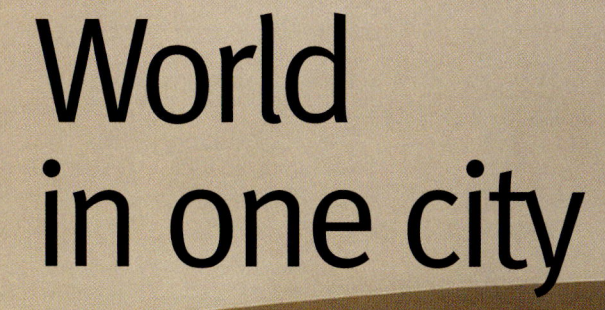

From South Carolina to the North West Frontier, an itsy-bitsy glimpse into Liverpool's global heritage...

Africa

■ Underneath one of the viewing platforms for the Piazza Waterfall at Beetham Plaza, there's a plaque in the shape of two tribal spears and a shield that commemorates the original 18th Century site of the arcaded warehouses of Goree Piazza, named after an island off the coast of Senegal. The Slave Trade funded Liverpool's phenomenal growth in that period, but its original black community – the oldest in Britain – is descended from African and American merchant seamen who married local women.

America

▢ No19 Abercromby Square, now University property near Hope Quarter, was once the home of Charles Prioleau, a Confederate businessman and secret agent during the American Civil War. Painted on the vestibule ceiling is a palmetto tree, the symbol of South Carolina (dating from 1776 when colonists in Charleston defended a fort built from palmetto logs against the British). On the ceilings of the old dining room are cherubs – one of them astride a wild turkey, the state's game-bird.

There's another turkey in the University's Art Gallery at no3 Abercromby Square, this one by wildlife painter John James Aubudon, a French-American who sailed from New Orleans to Liverpool in 1826.

His magnificent Birds of America book takes pride of place in Central Library's Picton Reading Room (see page 171). A collection of 435 hand-coloured engravings on the very large drawing paper known as double-elephant folio, it's one of only 133 copies of the most spectacular and valuable natural history book ever printed (four years ago one sold for £4.8million at Christie's in New York).

Canada

■ The Canada Dock Hotel on Regent Street (Central Docks) was built in 1860, seven years after the opening of the adjacent Canada Dock to handle North American timber. Standing on the gable of the pub is a lumberjack leaning on his axe, a faithful hound by his side. Liverpool had a shipping line called Canadian Pacific, and almost 500,000 emigrants sailed to Quebec from here.

Haiti

■ Above Hargreaves Building (now home the Racquet Club) on Chapel Street is a bust of Anacoana, 'the Golden Flower' – a Native American queen and heroine of anti-colonial resistance in Hispaniola. She and her Xaragua tribe were tricked and massacred by Spanish conquistadors in 1503.

World in one city

China

■ As early as 1834, the first vessel loaded with silk arrived in Liverpool direct from China, and for over a century the Blue Funnel Line was the premier Liverpool shipping company trading to China. By 1920 there were 14 places on Pitt Street (Rope Walks) where you could eat or buy Chinese food – a figure matched only by London's Limehouse. In 1953 Gladys Aylward founded the Liverpool Chinese Gospel Mission at 20 Nelson Street. Her story was told in the movie The Inn of Sixth Happiness, starring Ingrid Bergman and children from Liverpool's Chinatown and filmed in Bedgelert, North Wales.

India

■ There were Indian seafarers in Liverpool as long ago as the 1860s. The current community has it roots in a group who came from the Punjab in the early 1900s, long before the majority of Indians who arrived in the UK after 1950. Many became pedlars and established small businesses. Others worked in factories and supplemented their incomes as magicians or fortune-tellers. In 2002 the Museum of Liverpool Life presented The Indian Presence in Liverpool, a collection of personal histories and rare photos.

Greece

■ Liverpool's Greek community dates back to 1810 when a few merchants and cotton traders began operating from the port, with the Papayinnis shipping line founded 50 years later. The quadruple-domed Church of St Nicholas, built in 1870 on Berkley Street in Toxteth, was the second Greek Orthodox Church in England.

Israel

Liverpool's Jewish community is probably the oldest in the north of England, founded in the mid 18th Century by settlers from the Low Countries. The first synagogue was founded on Seel Street in 1807, the city elected its first Jewish mayor in 1863 and nine years later, at the height of Europe's fascination with Orientalism, one of the most beautiful synagogues in Anglo-Jewry was consecrated on Princes Road. A Jewish Heritage Trail is available from the Tourist Centres.

Sweden

Gustav Adolfs Kyrka, or the Scandinavian Seaman's Church (off Park Road), was built in 1884 by WD Caroe, son of the city's Danish consul and one of the most avant-garde architects of his day. Today it's owned by the Church of Sweden, with regular services in Swedish, Norwegian and Finnish.

Germany

The German Church on Canning Street was founded in the 1850s, and services are still held in the language. The Hahnemann Building on nearby Hope Street (now Liverpool School of Art & Design) was the first homeopathic hospital in Britain and named after Dresden's Samuel Hahnemann, the founder of holistic medicine.

Russia

There was a steady influx of Russian nationals to Liverpool in the early part of the last century, including the families of legendary opera singer Fyodor Chaliapin, decorated Black Sea navy admiral Pavel Nakhimov and even the tsarevitch Alexei's former nanny, all of whose descendants still live in the city.

World in one city

Wales

■ In Liverpool Town Hall are a couple of Bardic chairs (left) from the last two National Eisteddfods held in the city, in 1884 and 1900. Tens of thousands of Welsh people came to Liverpool in the late 18th Century – they even had their own Welsh newspaper – and the famous community in Patagonia came from a clipper that left Liverpool in 1865. In today's Toxteth there are streets called Geraint, Enid, Merlin, Modred, Elwy, Voelas, Rhiwlas, Gwydir and Pengwern.

Italy

■ The city's most famous Italian resident was novelist Rafael Sabatini, who lived at 47 Catharine Street in the 1920s and wrote swashbucklers like Scaramouche, Captain Blood and The Sea Hawk.

Ireland

■ Between 1849 and 1852 over 1.2million Irish emigrants arrived in Liverpool to escape famine back home, and there's a memorial in the grounds of St Luke's Church. The descendants of those who remained in the city have made an incalculable contribution to its multi-cultural heritage through all walks of life, and in 2004 a special CD-Rom was released to celebrate Liverpool's Irish ancestry.

France

■ Around 4,000 French prisoners were detained in Liverpool during the Napoleonic Wars (1772-1803). Those who died were buried in what is now St John's Gardens where a monument honours them.

Spain

■ On the pagoda in Roscoe Gardens (off Mount Pleasant) there's a plaque (right) from the city of Seville commemorating Jose Blanco White, the Spanish writer and political exile who worshipped at the Renshaw Street Unitarian Chapel (see pages 91 and 174) in the 1830s and is buried nearby.

What's to do...

■ A little bit of Mexico in the heart of Liverpool. Welcome to the Tavern Co, in Queen Square and on Allerton Road. The former is in an area of town dedicated to eating, drinking and generally having fun. Serving anything but traditional food, it offers a mouth-watering selection of spicy Mexican, Cajun and Tex-Mex delights in a colourful, welcoming and lively atmosphere that gets you right into the Latin spirit. A short taxi ride takes you to Allerton Road, a bustliing area packed with an eclectic mix of bars and restaurants. The Tavern Co here, a stone's throw from Penny Lane, is just as renowned for its excellent Mexican cuisine and enormous, sizzling steaks. A great place, too, to hit the tequila in true Mexicano style – without inflicting too much damage on your wallet.

107 **Advertorial**

Why pay for a hotel when what you need is a great stopover?

from just £25* per room per night

Travelodge is the leading budget stopover with over 240 locations throughout the UK and Ireland. Each spacious room contains an en-suite bathroom or shower room, a comfy king size bed, tea and coffee making facilities and colour TV. Family rooms can accommodate a family of 4 (up to 2 adults and 2 children under 16).

Travelodge has 2 ideally located lodges in Liverpool, so whether on business or leisure, taking a break in the city, or visiting family and friends, make Travelodge the first choice for your accommodation needs.

*£25 rate may not be available at every lodge, every night. £25 rates not commissionable. Cannot be used in conjunction with any offer or discount scheme and cannot be booked by phone.

The Liver Building

Liverpool Central

There is so much to do it is hard to know where to start! Ideally situated for all of the main activities in Liverpool and is only 5 minutes from Lime Street Station. Take your pick from dining out to shopping, museums to shows or maybe a trip to the famous Cavern Club. And, for all Liverpool and Everton supporters, the grounds are only a short distance away.

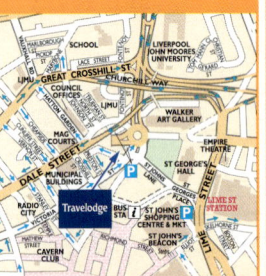

Liverpool Central
25 Old Haymarket
Liverpool
Merseyside L1 6ER

Tel: 0870 191 1656
Fax: 0151 227 5838

Liverpool Docks

Situated approx 1 mile from Albert Docks, offering the very best in culture in the North West! The Albert Docks is home to the Liverpool Tate for contemporary art, the Merseyside Maritime Museum, and 'The Beatles' experience. Amongst this hub of culture, there are also plenty of bars, shops and restaurants.

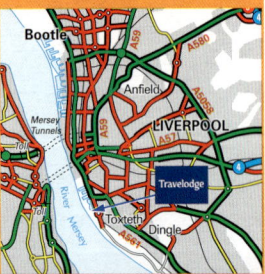

Liverpool Docks
Brunswick Dock
Sefton Street
Liverpool L3 4BN

Tel: 0870 191 1530
Fax: 0151 707 7769

For further information, or to make a booking contact the Travelodge team on

08700 850 950 or www.travelodge.co.uk

Travelodge

Room service

Where to stay. From luxury and boutique hotels to express and guesthouses…

■ You need somewhere to stay. You want contact details and some context – there's no point checking into a fab hotel if it's miles away from where you want to be. So whether you're coming to Liverpool for conferences or conventions, festivals or football matches, here's a little help.

The city centre offers old favourites like the Adelphi and unique newcomers like Hope Street Hotel, with a cluster of affordable options around Lime Street. The waterfront boasts a baker's dozen ranging from spectacular developments like Radisson SAS to express hotels in and around Albert Dock. (Express merely provides a more limited service, e.g. a bar but no restaurant). And in the suburbs you'll find a few absolute gems.

What's more, there may soon be a Malmasion at Princes Dock, Alias in Rope Walks, Hilton at Kings Dock and Beatles venue on Mathew Street. But that's then. This is now. Budget or boutique? Economy or sheer indulgence? And are you sure you still want that wake-up call?

Hotels

City centre

■ **Sir Thomas Hotel** ★★★
45 Victoria Street L1 6JB
Tel: (0151) 236 1366
Visit: newzbrasserie.com
Currently the closest hotel to the Beatles wonderland of Mathew Street, with a plush wine bar and restaurant downstairs. You'll be fascinated to know that it's also on the site of the Bank of Liverpool, the city's first joint-stock bank established in 1831.

■ **Travel Inn Metro** ★★★
Vernon Street L2 2AY
Tel: (0870) 238 3323
Visit: travelinn.co.uk
A new arrival in the Business (or recently renamed 'Live/Work') District of the city, linking Tithebarn and Dale Street and close to the Merseyrail station at Moorfields.

■ **Travelodge** ★★
25 Old Haymarket L1 6ER
Tel: 0870 191 1656
Visit: travelodge.co.uk
Bold and blue (main pic) and designed with real character by Urban Splash to the tune of £5million. Next to the Queensway tunnel entrance and a short walk to William Brown Street.

■ **Marriott City Centre** ★★★★
One Queen Square L2 1RH
Tel: (0151) 476 8000
Visit: marriott.com
Walk through Lime Street's sliding doors and there she blows, one of a high-density fusion of attractive, modern buildings (housing Italian, Chinese, Mexican and tapas restaurants, plus a cocktail bar and pub) that lie between the main shopping district and the cultural attractions of William Brown Street. Its Olivier's restaurant is an award-winner, and the Leisure Club has a swimming pool and spa bath.

■ **Gladstone Hotel** ★★★
Lord Nelson Street L3 5QB
Tel: (0151) 709 7050
Disembark at Lime Street and check in here within a matter of minutes (it's just a sharp right turn by the station's taxi-rank forecourt). Cosy and friendly and a favourite among regular visitors to the city.

■ **Holiday Inn** ★★★
Lime Street L1 1NQ
Tel: (0151) 709 7090
Visit: holiday-inn.com
Recently refurbished with meeting suites named after four of Liverpool's twin cities: Shanghai, Dublin, Cologne and New York.

■ **Adelphi Hotel** ★★★
Ranelagh Place L3 5UL
Tel: (0151) 709 7200
Visit: britanniahotels.com
Almost 200 years old and a legend in its own primetime as fans of the BBC docusoap will recall. In its early 20th Century heyday it was one of the most luxurious hotels in Europe and an arrival and departure point for transatlantic passengers (its Sefton Suite is a replica of the First Class Smoking Lounge on the Titanic). Today many of the rooms still feature solid marble walls and the original white marble swimming pool has been refurbished. A French restaurant, carvery and choice of bars, plus facilities for up to 800 guests, all a short walk from Lime Street.

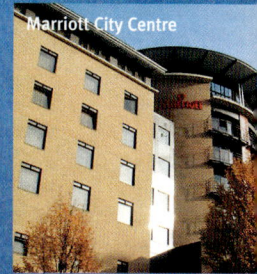
Marriott City Centre

Adelphi

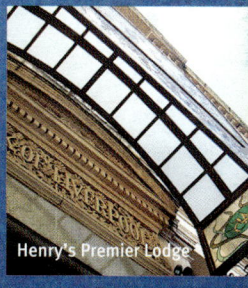
Henry's Premier Lodge

At your service...

■ Don't fancy a hotel? Try a four-star rated home from home instead. Days Serviced Apartments at Hatton Garden (close to the Cultural Quarter on William Brown Street) were designed by John Rocha, no less, and feature fully-equipped kitchens and secure parking. They're available for one night, a week or a month (0151 227 9467). Alternatively go for the Trafalgar Warehouse Apartments on Lord Nelson Street (back of Lime Street station, around the corner from the Empire Theatre), with brick walls, solid-wood surrounds and jacuzzis in an historic, Grade II listed building, or perhaps a Waterfront Penthouse on South Ferry Quay near Liverpool Marina (both 0845 601 1125).

■ **Aachen Hotel** ★★★
89-91 Mount Pleasant L3 5TB
Tel: (0151) 709 3633
Halfway up the hill towards the university complex is this friendly, affordable hotel with 17 rooms (nine en suite). Housed within a Grade II listed building and crowned 'The Place to Stay' at the prestigious North West Tourism Awards, it's been established for over 35 years. It's pronounced 'Arken', by the way, and named after the spa resort on the Dutch-German border.

Plucky little place

■ **Feathers Hotel** ★★★
117-125 Mount Pleasant L3 5TF
Tel: (0151) 709 9655
Visit: feathers.uk.com
Practically next door to the Aachen and providing standard rooms and luxury suites, all with satellite TV, 24-hour room service and a famous 'Eat As Much As You Like' breakfast.

■ **Hope Street Hotel** ★★★★
40 Hope Street L2 9DA
Tel: (0151) 709 3000
Visit: hopestreethotel.co.uk
The city's first luxury design hotel, independently-owned and located in the heart of Liverpool's theatreland (the Everyman, Philharmonic Hall and Unity are all nearby). As well as the London Carriage Works restaurant it boasts under-floor heating, king-size beds dressed in Egyptian cotton, bespoke contemporary furniture and rooms flooded by natural light through huge, arched windows. Each of the 48 rooms has a different view of the city – including the Albert Dock, Three Graces and the river – and there's a DVD/CD library, plasma-screen TV and broadband internet access. Already a favourite with visiting celebrities, and recently featured in the exclusive Design Hotels directory that lists 100 outstanding destination venues worldwide. Oh, and it houses the most extensive wine library outside London.

■ **Embassie Hostel** ★
1 Falkner Square L8 7NU
Tel: (0151) 707 1089
Visit: embassie.com
Formerly home to the Venezuelan consulate (built in 1820) and set in Liverpool's only complete Georgian square. The best accommodation for the budget traveller.

High on Hope

Hotels

Waterfront

The hotels...

1. Radisson SAS
2. Thistle
3. Racquet Club
4. Crowne Plaza
5. Trials
6. Moat House
7. Formule 1
8. Ibis
9. Premier Lodge
10. Express by Holiday Inn
11. Campanile
12. Dolby Hotel
13. Travelodge South

■ **Radisson SAS** ★★★★
105 Old Hall Street L3 9BS
Tel: (0151) 966 1500
Visit: radisson.com
An easy walk from the Pier Head to Liverpool's swankiest new hotel, part of a £60million flagship development featuring a 30-storey residential tower and 'urban art' gardens. The hotel's White Bar incorporates the front walls of two 200-year-old listed fishermen's cottages, and the cuisine in its 120-seater Filini restaurant is inspired by the produce of Sardinia.

■ **Thistle** ★★★★
Chapel Street L3 9RE
Tel: 0870 333 9137
Visit: thistlehotels.com/liverpool
Liverpool landmark in the shape of a ship, right on the Strand with great views of the river and Liver Building, and still known locally by its former name, the Atlantic Tower. A new twin-tower apartment development by Unity is taking shape next door, and the Racquet Club, historic Pig & Whistle pub and ancient Parish Church are within easy reach across Chapel Street.

■ **Racquet Club** ★★★★
Hargreaves Buildings,
5 Chapel Street L3 9AA
Tel: (0151) 236 6676
Visit: raquetclub.co.uk
A members club, conference centre, restaurant and art gallery rolled into one and run by brother-and-sister team, Martin and Helen Ainscough. As well as the eight rooms, all individually designed and decorated, there's a gym, sauna and plunge pool, plus squash courts and snooker tables. Ziba, the award-winning modern British restaurant, is downstairs. More or less opposite the Thistle Hotel, the building dates from 1859 with a frontage featuring busts of the world's greatest explorers. The paintings inside are taken from the Ainscough's private collection.

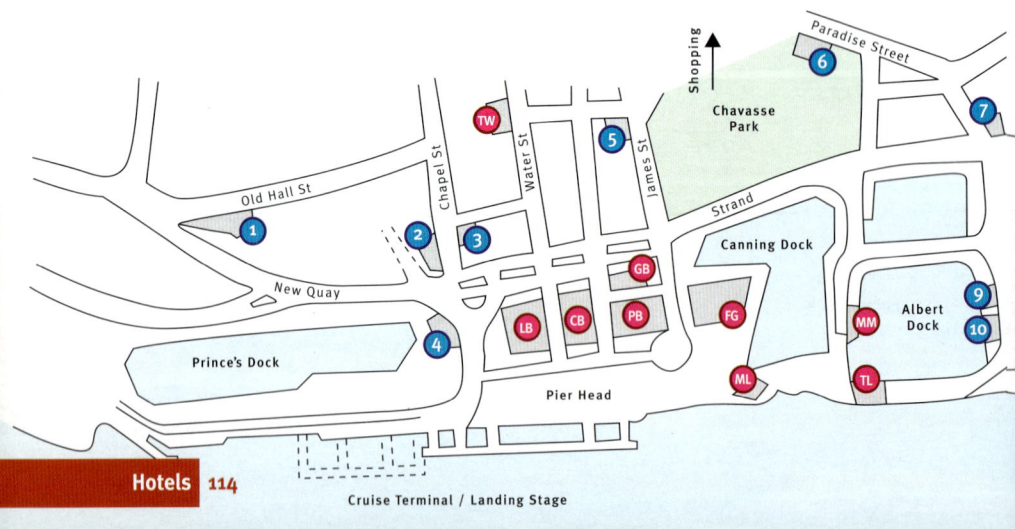

Hotels 114

■ **Crowne Plaza** ★★★★
St Nicholas Place,
Princes Dock L3 1QW
Tel: (0151) 243 8000
Visit: cpliverpool.com
Adjacent to the Liver Building, overlooking the river, and the place to spot a famous face – there always seem to be TV and sporting personalities in its Lounge Bar. Arguably the hotel with the best health and beauty facilities in the city: its Harbour Club has a gym, aerobic studio, heated swimming pool, jacuzzi, solarium, sauna and extensive range of beauty treatments.

■ **Trials** ★★★★
56-62 Castle Street L2 7LQ
Tel: (0151) 227 1021
Visit: trialshotel.com
Grade II listed, privately-owned hotel named after the nearby Queen Elizabeth II Law Courts and voted Cheshire Life's Liverpool Hotel of the Year 2003/04.

■ **Moat House** ★★★★
Paradise Street L1 8JD
Tel: (0151) 471 9988
Visit: moathousehotels.com
One of Liverpool's most famous and well-established hotels – although it's due to make way for the massive Grosvenor redevelopment of the entire Paradise Street and Chavasse Park district by the start of 2005. The dedicated conference centre has 14 meeting rooms catering for up to 600 people.

■ **Formule 1** ★★/Express
25 Wapping, Baltic Triangle L1 8LY
Tel: (0151) 709 2040
Visit: hotelformule1.com
'A good sleep in a pleasant and practical room'. That's the Formule 1 hotel chain motto. Modern and bright, with double beds and shared shower facilities, and one of several express hotels in and around the Albert Dock.

The attractions...

- TW Town Hall
- LB Liver Building
- CB Cunard Building
- GB George's Dock Building
- PB Port of Liverpool Building
- FG Fourth Grace Site
- ML Museum of Liverpool Life
- MM Maritime Museum
- TL Tate Liverpool
- KW King's Waterfront Site
- YH YHA Hostel
- LC Leo Casino
- CE Customs & Excise
- LM Liverpool Marina

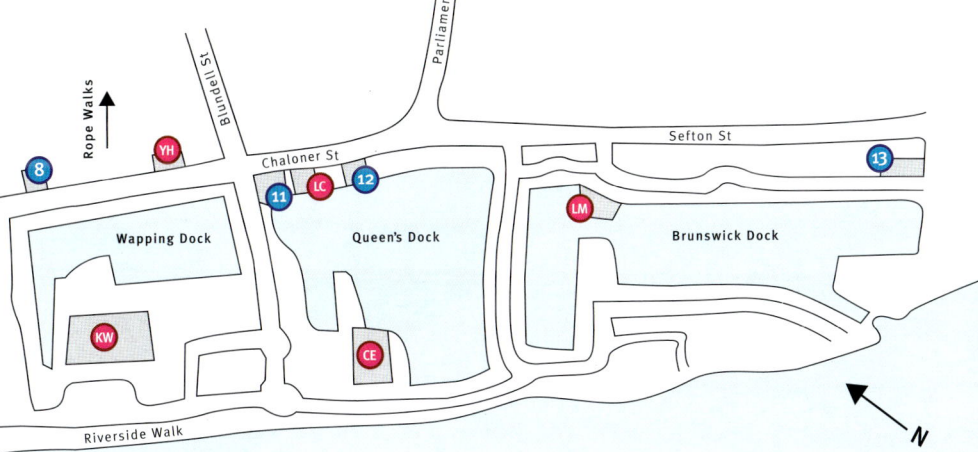

Hotels

Stargate SAS: the spectacular interior of the new Radisson on Old Hall Street

Hotels 116

■ **Ibis** ★★/Express
27 Wapping, Baltic Triangle L1 8DQ
Tel: **(0151) 706 9800**
Visit: **ibishotel.com**
Next door to Formule 1. Prides itself on solving problems in 15 minutes.

■ **Premier Lodge** ★★★
East Britannia Building,
Albert Dock L3 4AD
Tel: **0870 990 6432**
Visit: **premierlodge.com**
A handy Premier Lodge for Albert Dock tourists, opened in 2003 next door to the Beatles Story museum.

■ **Express by Holiday Inn**
★★★/Express
Britannia Pavillion,
Albert Dock L3 4AD
Tel: **(0151) 709 1133**
Visit: **hiexpress.com**
Incorporated into the Dock's existing structure. Handy for visits to the plush Pan American Club.

■ **Campanile** ★★/Express
Queens Dock L3 4AJ
Tel: **(0151) 709 8104**
Visit: **campanile.fr**
At night its green neon glows next to the Leo Casino's electric blue and pink (also owned by Amaury Taittinger, from the famous French champagne dynasty).

■ **Dolby** ★★/Express
Queens Dock L3 4DE
Tel: **(0151) 708 7272**
Visit: **dolbyhotels.co.uk**
Just turned 10 years old, and a favourite haunt for budget travellers. Over 60 rooms with satellite TV and ensuite shower.

■ **Travelodge South** ★★/Express
Brunswick Dock L3 4BH
Tel: **0870 191 1530.**
Visit: **travelodge.co.uk**
By Harry Ramsden's with a great view of the Marina and Graces.

Watch the birdies (and the fishies)...

■ Shock horror – you can still find hotels with that touch of individuality, not to mention the odd beautiful work of art and sculpture, in a big city like Liverpool. To truly appreciate Cormorants Diving (left), hanging in the lobby of the Thistle Hotel on Chapel Street, you have to visualise the ceiling level as the ocean surface with the birds diving through and disturbing shoals of fish. On the ceiling over at Trials on Castle Street there's an exquisite Liver Bird (right) amid the Victorian rococco decorations, while the entrance to Henry's Premier Lodge on Victoria Street has ornate lamps in the shape of orchids. Back on Chapel Street the huge canvas in the Racquet Club's restaurant, originally purchased at an auction in Antwerp, is a 19th-century copy of a medieval painting of the Medicis hunting. So now you know...

Hotels

Suburbs

North

■ **Royal Hotel** ★★★
Marine Terrace, Waterloo L22 5PR
Tel: (0151) 928 2332
Visit: liverpool-royalhotel.co.uk
Perfect for Aintree or the football. Well-equipped bedrooms and a refurbished Seabank Lounge with ultra-comfy leather chesterfields.

■ **Suites Hotel** ★★★★
Ribblers Lane, Knowsley,
Prescot L34 9HA
Tel: (0151) 549 2222
Presenting 80 rooms on four floors in one of the best business and banqueting venues in the North West. High-tech, high-spec.

■ **Devonshire House** ★★★
293-297 Edge Lane L7 9LD
Tel: (0151) 264 6600
Visit: devonshirehousehotel.com
More east than north (4km from city centre), a Georgian building within two acres of gardens. A la carte restaurant and a choice of seven conference rooms.

South

■ **Marriott South** ★★★★
Speke Aerodrome,
Speke Road L24 8QD
Tel: (0151) 494 5050
Visit: marriott.com
An unqualified success, three years after its conversion from the original Liverpool Airport terminal buildings with their stunning art deco architecture and interiors. Offers use of the adjacent David Lloyd leisure centre and complimentary shuttle service to JLA.

■ **Woolton Redbourne** ★★★★
Acrefield Road L25 5JN
Tel: 0845 601 1125
Visit: merseyworld.com/woolton-redbourne
Celeb-friendly venue with a restaurant open to non-residents. Originally a country house designed by a Victorian industrialist, it's set amid landscaped gardens with rooms furnished in period style and an imaginative table d'hôte.

■ **Alicia Hotel** ★★★
3 Aigburth Drive L17 3AA
Tel: (0151) 727 4411
Beautifully illuminated on the boulevard encircling Sefton Park, and top service around the clock.

■ **Blenheim Lodge** ★★★
37 Aigburth Drive,
Sefton Park L17 4JE
Tel: (0151) 727 7380
Spacious, privately-run guesthouse on the Beatles trail as the former digs of Stuart Sutcliffe.

■ **Park Lane Hotel** ★★★
23 Aigburth Drive L17 4JQ
Tel: (0151) 727 4754
Hotel dating back to the 18th Century and tastefully refurbished.

The young ones...

■ Liverpool's YHA hostel (0870 770 5924) is in its own secure area on Wapping (opposite Brunswick Dock) with the historic Baltic Fleet pub, swinging Blundell Street bar and restaurant and a good old-fashioned McDonald's for company. As usual there's 24-hour access, onsite parking (with room for two coaches) and all rooms are ensuite (multi-share for 3,4 or 6).
By general consent the self-catering kitchen is excellent, and there's a café area for evening meals plus a games room and TV lounge with Beatles decor and usually a good mix of world travellers.

Illuminating Alicia

Wherever your travelling takes you, at Travel Inn, you can be sure of good quality spacious rooms and comfortable surroundings, to ensure you get the good night's sleep you need.

At every Travel Inn you'll find:
- Comforable 'Hypnos' king sized beds
- Good quality duvets and pillows
- Temperature control facility
- Ensuite bathrooms with bath and shower
- Remote control TV and radio alarm
- Spacious desk area should you need to work
- Tea and coffee making facilities

There will also be a room to suit your needs, whether you're away with the family and need a family room, you require a smoking room or have a disability and require a spacially designed room to make your stay more comfortable.

Whatever your reason for staying away, you can be sure that Travel Inn provides everything you want for a good nights sleep.

Travel Inn Aintree
1 Ormskirk Road
Aintree
Liverpool L9 5AS
Tel. 08701 977 157

Liverpool North Travel Inn
North Perimeter Road
Bootle
Liverpool L30 7PT
Tel. 08701 977 158

Liverpool Tarbock
Wilson Road
Tarbock
Liverpool
L36 6AD
Tel. 08701 977 159

Liverpool West Derby Travel Inn
Queens Drive
West Derby
Liverpool L13 0DL
Tel. 08701 977 160

City Centre Travel Inn
Vernon Street
Liverpool L2 2AY
Tel. 0870 238 3323

www.travelinn.co.uk - Central reservations number 0870 242 8000

How far? From your hotel to

Hotels	Restaurants	London C/W	Tea Factory	Heathcotes	Ziba	60 Hope Street	Ego	Lower Place	Everyman	Pierre Victoire	Puschka	Other Place	Baby Cream	Blue Bar	Honey Harmony	Living Room	Newz Bar	Pacific Bar
Sir Thomas										Walkable						Doorstep		
Travel Inn																Walkable	Walkable	
Travelodge HM																Walkable	Walkable	
Marriott										Walkable						Doorstep		
Gladstone																		
Holiday Inn		Walkable	Walkable			Walkable	Walkable	Walkable		Walkable		Walkable	Walkable			Walkable		
Adelphi																		
Aachen		Doorstep	Doorstep			Doorstep	Doorstep	Doorstep	Walkable	Walkable	Doorstep							
Feathers		Doorstep				Walkable	Walkable	Walkable	Walkable	Walkable	Doorstep							
Hope Street		Doorstep				Walkable	Walkable	Walkable	Walkable	Walkable	Doorstep							
Embassie		Walkable				Walkable	Walkable	Walkable		Walkable								
Radisson				Walkable													Walkable	
Thistle				Walkable	Doorstep												Walkable	
Racquet Club				Walkable														
Crowne Plaza				Walkable	Doorstep													
Trials																Walkable	Walkable	
Moat House			Walkable	Walkable				Walkable				Walkable	Walkable					
Formule 1				Walkable									Walkable					
Ibis				Walkable									Walkable					
Premier Lodge AD				Walkable									Doorstep	Doorstep				
Express H/Inn				Walkable									Doorstep	Doorstep				
Campanile																		
Dolby																		
Travelodge South																		

■ Doorstep   ■ Walkable   □ Wheels

Hotels 120

the nearest good restaurant?

Colin's Bridewell · Slaughterhouse · Jenny's · Ask · Casa Italia · Est Est Est · Franco's · Villa Romana · Mayflower · Orchid Spring · Sapporo · Yuet Ben · Shere Khan · Sultan's Palace · El Macho · Pan American · Valparaiso · Al Andalus · Algarve · Don Pepe · La Tasca · St Petersburg · Christakis

■ Use the grid to find the nearest restaurant to where you're staying. All 40 of them are featured overleaf...

Restaurants

prohibition
COCKTAIL BAR - RESTAURANT - CLUB
1A BOLD STREET, LIVERPOOL, L1 4DJ. T.0870 44 22 860
liverpool@prohibition.uk.com - www.prohibition.uk.com

Ready to order

The best cuisine in Liverpool. From around the world with love

■ The lunchtime menu at Colin's Bridewell, a gastropub in a converted police station in Rope Walks, says it all: Thai green curry, ratatouille, hoi sin duck tortilla, Greek feta salad, penne pasta with smoked bacon, chicken, red chillies and goats cheese. Whatever you want to eat you'll find it in Liverpool, a city whose impressive variety of cuisine reflects its rich multi-cultural heritage.

There are the aesthetics of dining out to consider, too. Choose modern British cooking in minimalist steel-and-glass venues on the waterfront, authentic Russian food in the raucous environs of Rope Walks, sophisticated international cuisine in the city's theatreland, and just about everything in-between.

The following 40 restaurants may be just a selection, but they represent (in our humble opinion) a reasonable cross-section of what to expect. There are good modern venues at Queen Square in the Retail Centre (close to Lime Street, the museums and galleries of William Brown Street and the Empire and Royal Court Theatres), a stretch of fabulous establishments in the Hope Quarter, and numerous lounge-bar options around the Business District and Albert Dock. And that's not including the dim-sum delights of Chinatown and abundance of cool cafés.

You're salivating, we can tell...

Restaurants

International

■ **London Carriage Works** HQ
40 Hope Street L2 9DA
Tel: **(0151) 709 3000**
Visit: **hopestreethotel.co.uk**
First impression: wow. Serving modern international cuisine on the ground floor of the Hope Street Hotel and striving for what they call 'perfect execution in a fast-moving kitchen to capture the conviviality of good food, good wine and good company'. The name comes from the building's original function as a warehouse where coaches were built and repaired.

■ **Tea Factory Bar & Kitchen** RW
Fleet Street (next to FACT) L1 4DQ
Tel: **(0151) 708 7008**
Opened last May, this a relaxed environment with an eye-catching mural (left) depicting Liverpool's historic trade routes – a theme repeated in the 'global tapas' at the bar. The mezzanine restaurant has a 'theatre' of an open kitchen.

Location key:

PH Pier Head/Albert Dock
BD Business District
SC Shopping Centre
CQ Cultural Quarter
RW Rope Walks
HQ Hope Quarter

European

■ **60 Hope Street HQ**
60 Hope Street L1 9BZ
Tel: (0151) 707 6060
Visit: 60hopestreet.com
You'd be hard-pressed to find a more elegant dining venue anywhere else in the country let alone Liverpool, nor a better menu. Honoured as one of top 10 new eateries outside London in the Restaurant Remys awards, and patronised by Bob Hoskins and Samuel L Jackson among others.

■ **Ego HQ**
57 Hope Street L1 9BW
Tel: (0151) 706 0707
Visit: egorestaurants.com
Feel like you're back on holiday? Good, that's the idea. The decor is very terracotta and the seasonal menu is based on what they call 'rustic Mediterranean cuisine', sourced direct from the region and featuring some cracking seafood dishes.

■ **The Lower Place HQ**
Philharmonic Hall,
Hope Street L1 9BP
Tel: (0151) 210 1955
Visit: liverpoolphil.com/rlpo/lower
The Phil's basement eaterie was Cheshire Life Restaurant of the Year 2002/03. It's also Good Food Guide-listed. And the Queen's dined there. There are tapas nights to coincide with performances, and the table d'hote menu has a £10-for-two courses offer. For example, horseshoe black pudding, apple-and-date chutney and game chips, then lamb cutlets with roast potatoes, and with red wine jus.

Ziba: the art of modern British cuisine

British

■ **Simply Heathcotes BD**
Beetham Plaza,
25 The Strand L2 0XL
Tel: (0151) 236 3536
Visit: heathcotes.co.uk
Modern British cuisine at its best – check out Paul Heathcote's award-winning roast breast of Goosnargh duck – with a special offers on Monday nights featuring a choice of selected a la carte dishes and free bottle of Chilean red or white.

■ **Ziba @ The Racquet Club BD**
Hargreaves Building,
5 Chapel Street L3 9AG
Tel: (0151) 236 6676
Visit: racquetclub.co.uk
An old favourite relocated from the edge of Chinatown to Liverpool's premier boutique hotel on the banks of the Mersey (well, almost). The cuisine is modern British and the head chef is a former Conran cook. Culinary class guaranteed.

Bistros

■ **Everyman Bistro HQ**
Everyman Theatre,
9-11 Hope Street L1 9BH
Tel: (0151) 708 9545
Visit: everyman.co.uk
A regular in food and wine guides and the only venue to receive an A* in the Observer/Harden guide for great value and atmosphere.

■ **Pierre Victoire SC**
14 Button Street L2 6PS
Tel: (0151) 227 2577
The little corner of Liverpool that's forever Paris, in a converted warehouse just around the corner from Ted Baker in the Cavern Quarter. Mussels in white wine are a speciality.

■ **Puschka HQ**
16 Rodney Street L1 2TE
Tel: (0151) 708 8698
Outstanding example of How To Get It Right. And participating in the 2004 Liverpool Biennial with an 'Art in the Bar' exhibition.

■ **The Other Place HQ**
29A Hope Street L1 9BQ
Tel: (0151) 707 7888
Intimate little eaterie on the same block as the Everyman and Casa.

Hotels

■ **The Brasserie @ Crowne Plaza PH**
2 St Nicholas Place,
Princes Dock L3 1QW
Tel: (0151) 243 8000
Visit: cpliverpool.com
Contemporary international dishes from the one of the city's poshest hotels. And a great breakfast.

■ **Filini @ Radisson PH**
105 Old Hall Street L3 9BS
Tel: (0151) 966 1500
Visit: radisson.com
Opened on Valentine's Day 2004 and inspired by the best of Sardinian cuisine, with an exclusively Italian wine list.

■ **Olivier's @ Marriott City SC**
Queen Square L1 1RH
Tel: (0151) 476 8000
Visit: marriott.com
You can tell it's somewhere swanky when Sir Larry's plastered all over the walls and the menu has 'To Commence' at the top. But there's 'traditional Scouse' as well as sautéed chicken livers to choose from.

Where to get great...

- Griddled tuna steak with nicoise salad ...... 3345 Parr Street
- Grilled steaks of wild boar ...... Algarve
- Roast rump of lamb with bubble and squeak ...... 60 Hope Street
- Calzone with mozzarella and chopped ham ...... Al Andalus
- Fish, chips and mushy peas ...... Newz Bar
- Charcoal-grilled swordfish & salmon skillet ...... El Macho
- Barbary toffee duck apples with marmalade pork ribs ...... Baby Cream
- Whole sea bass with parsley, fennel and tarragon ...... Villa Romana
- Barbecued skewers of monkfish and smoked cod ...... Puschka
- Thai red curry chicken with coconut milk ...... Orchid Spring
- Roasted red pepper risotto with spinach and truffle ...... St Petersburg
- Vietnamese hot and sour beef and pak choi noodles ...... Tea Factory

What's to do...

■ Where you're a guest at our stunning Radisson SAS hotel or not, Filini is definitely worth sampling. There's been nothing like this in Liverpool before – superb Sardinian cuisine in an environment emulating the style of Locanda Locatelli. Our Rapido menu features dishes like pancetta and fig salad with balsamic vinegar, followed by mussels steamed with broccoli and crushed thyme potatoes, and finishing with baked ricotta and pine nut tart. For a more leisurely meal, how about air-dried wild boar with celery and endive, marinated sambuca pork belly with gremolata potatoes, ending with chocolate risotto with orange creme fraiche? hatever you decide upon, your tatse buds are in for a treat.

Café society

That'll be an unleaded mochaccino without. And make it tall with wings...

Culture to go?
- **Bluecoat Café Bar**, School Lane. Picnic benches in the courtyard, art for sale.
- **Café Eros**, Conservation Centre, Whitechapel. Fully-licensed table service amid the latest laser technology.
- **Café Maritime**, Albert Dock. Hot and cold meals at the Maritime Museum.
- **Anglican Cathedral Refectory**, St James Mount. Delicious home-cooked food.
- **FACT Café**, Wood Street. Appetisers among the art installations.
- **Liverpool Museum Café**, William Brown Street. Top sandwiches and desserts.
- **Taste Café**, Tate Liverpool, Albert Dock. Modern British food on the menu (and occasionally on the walls).
- **Walker Café**, William Brown Street. Tapas and refreshments.

■ People passing by, seagulls wheeling overhead. Offenbach (ahem) drifting over the reassuring gush of an espresso machine, and the delicious aroma of roasted arabica beans. You're in Caffé Nero on Castle Street, possibly, or Starbucks a few doors down. Either way you're hanging out in one of downtown Liverpool's top cafés.

Other favourites in the Business District include Café Connect on Old Hall Street, one of the first continental cafés in the city, and the spacious Expresso Exchange on Victoria Street, a happy mix of busy professionals and window-seat daydreamers.

Puccino's on Mathew Street is the most popular café in Beatles territory, thanks to its friendly service and splendid range of smoothies, and in Rope Walks look out for Hemingways on Lower Duke Street, currently serving up award-winning Antica Tostatura Triestina coffee while customers play chess or backgammon.

A little up the hill on Parr Street (off Upper Duke Street), 3345 is a recording studio complex with a 'lounging restaurant'. And over on Bold Street, four of the best hang-outs are Tabac (legendary sandwiches), the Soul Café (lazy jazz grooves and Memphis Stew), Caffé D'Oro (famed for its funky décor and formidable breakfasts) and Maggie May's (cosy seats, traditional home-made cooking).

"Don't look now, but there's a strange bloke standing there with a camera..."

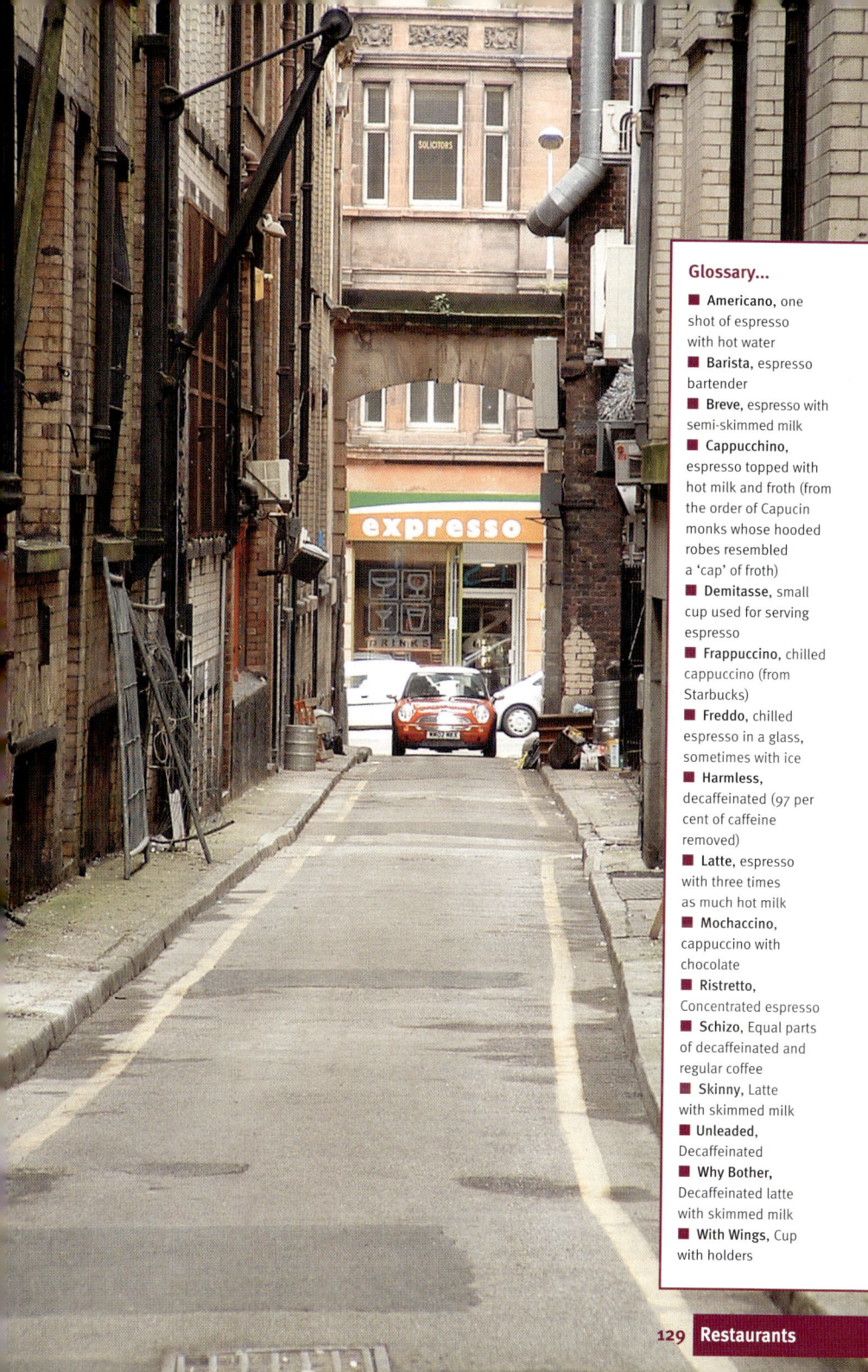

Glossary...

- **Americano,** one shot of espresso with hot water
- **Barista,** espresso bartender
- **Breve,** espresso with semi-skimmed milk
- **Cappucchino,** espresso topped with hot milk and froth (from the order of Capucin monks whose hooded robes resembled a 'cap' of froth)
- **Demitasse,** small cup used for serving espresso
- **Frappuccino,** chilled cappuccino (from Starbucks)
- **Freddo,** chilled espresso in a glass, sometimes with ice
- **Harmless,** decaffeinated (97 per cent of caffeine removed)
- **Latte,** espresso with three times as much hot milk
- **Mochaccino,** cappuccino with chocolate
- **Ristretto,** Concentrated espresso
- **Schizo,** Equal parts of decaffeinated and regular coffee
- **Skinny,** Latte with skimmed milk
- **Unleaded,** Decaffeinated
- **Why Bother,** Decaffeinated latte with skimmed milk
- **With Wings,** Cup with holders

Restaurants

What's to do...

■ Welcome to Bluu Liverpool, with cousins in Hoxton Square and Nottingham. We're in the Tea Factory in Rope Walks and we're 926sq metres of good times, guaranteed. We've got upstairs and basement bars, a dance area and VIP bar, and a 60-seater restaurant that's light and comfortable – reflecting our ethos to provide fine dining without any stuffiness. Relax in our retro furniture, watch our chefs at work or admire the floral designs of our murals before consulting our fabulous menu. For example: half-a-dozen rock oysters in red wine and shallot vinegar, Cornish lemon sole with musroom and herb crust and spinach-bashed potatoes, and capuccino ice-cream with homemade macaroons. Enjoy...

Lounge

■ **Baby Cream PH**
Suite 4M, Atlantic Pavilion,
Albert Dock L3 4AE
Tel: (0151) 702 5823
Visit: babycream.co.uk
More intimate Cream venue that's updated the 70s fondue style to incorporate flavours from around the globe, 'to tear and share'.

■ **Blue Bar & Grill PH**
Edward Pavilion,
Albert Dock L3 4AB
Tel: (0151) 709 7097
Visit: lyceumgroup.co.uk/bluebar
A mezzanine-based grill – featuring US fusion cooking and modern British dishes – and 'a great place to sample the new Liverpool' (Harpers & Queen magazine).

■ **Honey Harmony SC**
Queen Square, Great Charlotte Street L1 1RH
Tel: (0151) 709 3933
Visit: honeyharmony.co.uk
Unpretentious cuisine, and a lunchtime favourite with city professionals.

■ **The Living Room BD**
15 Victoria Street L2 5QS
Tel: (0151) 236 1999
Visit: thelivingroom.co.uk
Arguably the classiest hang-out in town – dig that grand piano – with a cool, airy interior and excellent a la carte grill menu.

■ **Newz Brasserie BD**
18 Water Street L2 0TD
Tel: (0151) 236 2025
Visit: newzbrasserie.com
Walk off Water Street into a dark, cavernous world with sweeping curtains and huge jeroboams.

It's like something out of an Anne Rice novel, only with more footballers and soap stars. The split-level restaurant was recently honoured as one of the country's top 10 eateries by Glamour magazine.

■ **Pacific Bar & Grill BD**
Pacific Chambers,
Temple Street L2 5RH
Tel: (0151) 236 0270
Visit: pacificbarandgrill.com
In the Reef restaurant in the basement, the main menu is a fusion of Pacific Rim cuisine. All housed in one of Liverpool's most beautiful neo-classical buildings.

Gastropubs

■ **Colin's Bridewell RW**
Campbell Street L1 5BL
Tel: (0151) 707 8003
Located in a former police station. The cuisine – from Afro-Caribbean to Chinese – reflects Liverpool's rich seafaring heritage. Simple food laced with sophistication.

■ **The Courtyard BD**
19 Dale Street L2 2EZ
Tel: (0151) 236 5556
Global cuisine and exposed bricks and beams in the Rigby's Building.

■ **The Slaughterhouse BD**
13-15 Fenwick Street L2 7LS
Tel: (0151) 231 6881
Visit: laughterhouse.com
They buy six pieces of fresh cod every morning, dip them in batter and fry to order. Result: sensational fish and (home-made) chips.

Honey pot

Fair cop

Restaurants

Italian

■ **ASK SC**
Queen Arcade,
Queen Square L1 1FS
Tel: (0151) 709 0080
Visit: askcentral.co.uk
It's 10 years since the team behind ASK (the initials of directors Adam and Sam Kaye) opened their first restaurant in Belsize Park, north London. They have a penchant for moving into restored or listed buildings, but their Liverpool premises are in a more contemporary setting.
The food? Deliciously Italian.

■ **Casa Italia BD**
40 Stanley Street L1 6AL
Tel: (0151) 227 5774
Visit: thecasaitalia.co.uk
A family-run fixture for the best part of 25 years on the Liverpool restaurant scene and a perennial award winner. Unbeatable value for money in an authentic trattoria.

■ **Franco's @ Bar Italia BD**
48A Castle Street L2 2LQ
Tel: (0151) 236 3375
A taste of the Eternal City. Try the gamberoni alla Franco – the head chef's king prawn secret recipe.

■ **Olive Press Pizzeria BD**
25-27 Castle Street L2 4TA
Tel: (0151) 227 2242
Those live Canadian lobsters are fresh from Fleetwood. There's Peroni on draught. And hand-made artisan pasta, stone-baked pizzas and some lovely brick-fired dishes.

■ **Villa Romana RW**
6-8 Wood Street L1 4AQ
Tel: (0151) 708 8004
A busy restaurant on the fringe of the city's bacchic clubland, it still manages to ooze laid-back charm and sophistication. Ever-dependable antipasti dishes and lemon sole that melts in the mouth.

Seafood

■ **Jenny's Seafood Restaurant BD**
The Old Ropery,
Fenwick Street L2 7NB
Tel: (0151) 236 0332
Established for 40 years, on an alley just down the side of the Britannia Buildings off Fenwick Street (that's off Water Street). Walk down the steep wooden staircase and step back in time. Established for 40 years, this is the very model of old-school restaurant propriety, with impeccably-attired staff and wonderfully prepared and presented food. Fortunately the prices aren't so exclusive.

Yes yes yes

■ **Est Est Est PH**
Edward Pavillion,
Albert Dock L3 4AF
Tel: (0151) 408 6969
When was the last time you sat down to a really good spatchcock poussin? Just one of the highlights of the menu in the light, bright Albert Dock favourite (above).

What's to do...

■ Vue Bar & Grill, on Campbell Square (off Lower Duke Street) is one of Rope Walk's newest and most stylish venues, boasting exclusivity combined with great food and drink, and excellent service and locality. A simple pasta dish and a glass of fine wine, or a full-course meal in your favourite restaurant? Your choices at the Vue are endless, and frequent menu changes keep our customers pleasantly surprised and always satisfied. There's live jazz music, too, every Sunday evening from 8pm, plus special three-course offers Sunday through to Thursday. Vue Bar & Grill's dedication to quality, wholesome and simple food is paramount. Why not join us and enjoy our service?

133 **Advertorial**

South Asian

Enter the dragon

■ At the last count there were 17 restaurants in Liverpool's Chinatown (in Rope Walks), most of them on Nelson Street with a few on nearby Berry Street. Of course, there are other great Chinese venues outside the district, notably Chung Ku on Riverside Drive (vaunted in The Good Food Guide for its excellent dim sum range), Tai Pan on Great Howard Street (one of the Observer Food Monthly magazine's top five Chinese restaurants in the country) and May Sum in St John's Precinct (Liverpool's biggest eat-as-much-as-you-like buffet restaurant). And back in Chinatown two great supermarkets to explore: Hondo on Upper Duke Street (by Yuet Ben), and Chung Wah on the corner of Hardy Street and St James Street.

■ **Shere Khan** RW
17-19 Berry Street L1 4SD
Tel: (0151) 709 6099
One of a chain of seven curry houses owned by millionaire restauranteur Nighat Awan and marketing itself as 'the McDonald's of Indian food'. Modern decor, and you can purchase sauces and pickles for sale at the counter.

■ **Sultan's Palace** BD
75-77 Victoria Street L2 6TN
Tel: (0151) 227 9020
Opulent basement restaurant with chefs poached from five-star hotels in Delhi to create the very best Indian food. Low-fat, healthy dishes prepared in a tandoor oven. The fish kofta comes highly recommended.

South East Asian

■ **Mayflower** RW
48 Duke Street L1 5AS
Tel: (0151) 709 6339
Visit: index.force9.co.uk/mayflower
Dishes from Peking, Canton and Szechuan. After an extensive refurbishment it now boasts two floors and a private suite for parties and functions. And just look at the size of those banquets.

■ **Orchid Spring** SC
47 Paradise Street L1 3BP
Tel: (0151) 708 8400
A shangri-la of Thai cuisine on Paradise Street, one down from Radio Merseyside, and a big hit with clock-watching office workers at lunchtime. Who says tapas has to be Spanish? A typical Thai meal consists of hot, spicy, sweet and sour dishes that'll have you hooked.

■ **Sapporo Teppanyaki** RW
134 Duke Street,
East Village L1 5AG
Tel: (0151) 705 3005
Visit: sapporoteppanyaki.com
Sushi and noodle café-bar showcasing the delights of theatre cooking: a chef is assigned to each table as diners watch their food being prepared. On the ground floor of Hudson Gardens in an area earmarked as the city's premier restaurant quarter.

■ **Yuet Ben** RW
1 Upper Duke Street L1 9DU
Tel: (0151) 709 5772
Visit: yuetben.merseyworld.com
A fixture in the city for 35 years and a favourite among discerning lovers of Chinese food. Simple, intimate and self-styled as 'Liverpool's first and original Peking-style restaurant'. Yuet Ben means 'Honoured Guest'.

Orchid Spring: Shangri-la on Paradise Street

Restaurants 134

Restaurants

Estuvo delicioso...

Iberian

■ **Al Andalus** BD
2 Brunswick Street L2 0PL
Tel: (0151) 236 0137
Tucked away opposite Beetham Plaza for the best part of 15 years, and one of 10 Spanish restaurants in the UK recommended by the Guardian who say, 'If you and your friends want to enjoy Spanish cooking at its finest, this is the place to come'.

Americas

■ **El Macho** HQ
23 Hope Street L1 9BQ
Tel: (0151) 708 6644
Visit: elmachorestaurants.co.uk
Opened in 1985 by two brothers from Baja. Well-known for its pueblo-style interior, great atmosphere and fantastic skillets and charcoal-grilled steaks.

■ **Pan American Club** PH
22 Britannia Pavilion,
Albert Dock L3 4EF
Tel: (0151) 709 7097
Visit: lyceumgroup.co.uk/panamerican
Award-winning interior housed in the old This Morning studios. Traditional American cuisine presented with the panache of a Parisian brasserie.

■ **Valparaiso** HQ
4 Hardman Street L1 9AX
Tel: (0151) 708 6036
Visit: valparaiso-restaurant.co.uk
Minced beef topped with sweetcorn or seafood paella with saffron rice? The menu at Liverpool's only Chilean restaurant, established back in 1985, presents you with delicious dilemmas.

■ **Algarve** BD
20 Stanley Street L1 6AF
Tel: (0151) 236 0206
Visit: algarverestaurant.co.uk
Authentic Portuguese restaurant with a special banquet offer from Monday to Thursday featuring sardines, omelette, grilled lamb chop, chicken piri, fried crab claws, mussels, mushrooms, french fries and garlic bread. And an espresso!

■ **Don Pepe** BD
Union House,
19-21 Victoria Street L1 6BD
Tel: (0151) 231 1909
Independent Spanish venue with charming waiting-on service. The succulent steak and rich vegetarian paella options give this well-established place the classy reputation it deserves. Dig the huge central fountain.

■ **La Tasca** SC
3 Queen Square L1 1RH
Tel: (0151) 709 1070
Big, lively tapas bar behind the Marriott Hotel. Most of the staff are Spanish, and the dishes are traditional and tasty. A great place to eat al fresco (and drink Spanish-brewed San Miguel) weather permitting.

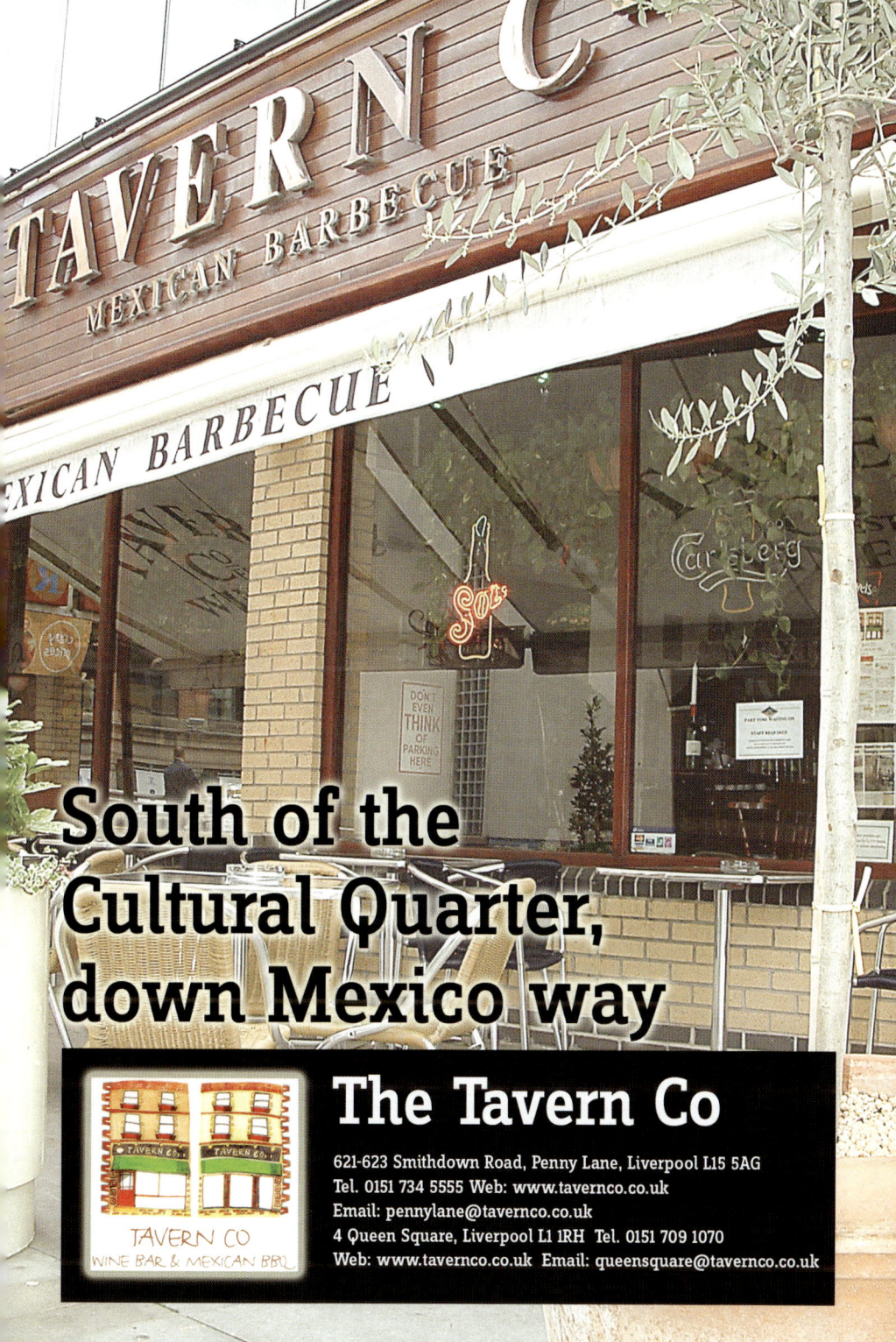

MUSTARD
RESTAURANT & BAR

Pleasurable

Satisfying

Fragrant

Delightful

Delicious

Melodious

Mustard Restaurant & Bar, 336 - 338 Smithdown Road Liverpool L15 2HD
For information and bookings please call 0151 222 1123
or visit www.mustardrestaurantandbar.co.uk

FAITH IN ONE CITY 2004

Russian

■ **St Petersburg RW**
7A York Street L1 5BN
Tel: **(0151) 709 6676**
Visit: **st-petersburg.virtualave.net**
The only authentic Russian restaurant outside London. There are a dozen types of blini (pancakes with delicious fillings) alone on the menu, as well as 13 home-made soups and over 30 cold appetisers including caviar and beluga. That's before you come to the main courses. Eight beef options at the last count, among them the sumptuous goviadina po gusarsky (grilled fillet steak stuffed with mushrooms and baked in pastry to an old Russian recipe). Dishes from the Russian Federation plus all 15 former Soviet republics are represented on the menu. There's a pervasive French influence, too, harking back to the Francophile tastes of the Russian imperial family. And the chandelier, in case you're wondering, is from St Petersburg, too.

Greek

■ **Christakis Taverna RW**
7 York Street L1 5BN
Tel: **(0151) 708 7377**
Visit: **christakisgreektaverna.com**
A cracking venue below St Petersburg on York Street (second right from the bottom of Duke Street, close to Colin's Bridewell). The building is over 200 years old and it's housed a Greek restaurant for 30 of them. Countless courses, generous helpings and, of course, lots of dancing and plate smashing. A great night-out.

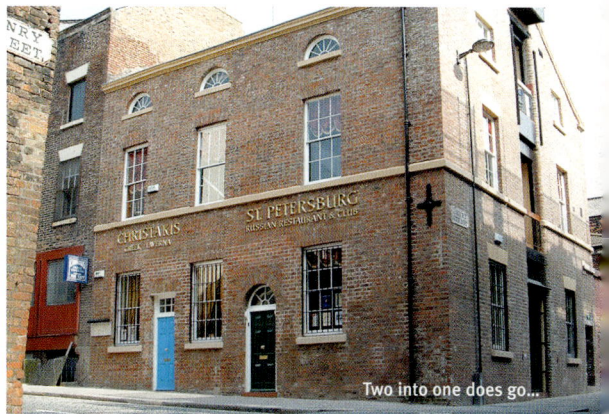
Two into one does go...

North end...

■ **Charlie Parker's (0151 928 1101)** on Waterloo's Crosby Road North has earned a word-of-mouth reputation for its welcoming atmosphere and legendary Thai fishcakes. On nearby Church Road there's **Touchwood Bar (0151 928 5656)**, a lounge venue that serves 'peewack', a traditional Scouse soup made of lentils and bacon ribs, and hosts salsa nights. As does **The Eating Room (01704 873735)** at Shorrocks Hill Country Club on Formby's Lifeboat Road. It's an international restaurant in a beautiful hotel and health club complex used by current and former top footballers.

South end...

■ Lark Lane in Aigburth is a bohemian outpost bursting with good restaurants. **Maranto's (0151 727 7200)** is admired for its American steak dishes, while at French bistro **L'Alouette (0151 707 8123)** tables by the open fire should be booked for free. The candlelit cosiness comes for free. **Que Pasa Cantina (0151 727 0006)** serves burritos, fajitas and lashings of Mexican beer, and **Esteban (0151 727 6056)** is a busy tapas bar. There's an open kitchen at Greek restaurant **Romio's (0151 727 7252)**, global fusion at **Viva (0151 726 0160)** and elegant homeliness about **Keith's Wine Bar (0151 728 7688)**. All down the one street.

Nearby Aigburth Road boasts **Gulshan (0151 427 1323)**, recognised by the Michelin Guide and listed as one of the top 50 curry houses in the country by The Independent, while Allerton Road has the seafood specialities of **Fusion (0151 724 6070)**, international tapas of **Pod (0151 724 2255)** and Vietnamese delights of **Fung Lok (0151 722 9560)**. Towards town along Smithdown Road there's modern British cooking at **Jalons Wine Bar (0151 734 0329)**, more global fusion at **Mustard (0151 222 2466)** and Thai delights at **Siam Garden (0151 734 1871)**.

food

A Lá Carté available using fresh local produce
Lounge menu available all day

drink

Extensive, award-winning cocktail selection
Plus huge selection of wines and beers

music

Basement music venue featuring
live bands and club nights

bluu

Maker's Mark

St. Peter's Square, Fleet Street, Liverpool, L1 4DQ
Tel. 0151 709 8462   Fax. 0151 709 6663   Email: liverpool@bluu.co.uk

In association with:

All bar none

You're in clubbing paradise. Unless you fancy a quiet pint. Same again?

■ Where's the action? Depends what you're after. Down on the Albert Dock you'll find some of Liverpool's hippest bars. Further south, the high-rolling Leo Casino and Rat Pack-tastic Blundell Street.

Let's go the other way, across The Strand to Cooper's 'Good Time' Emporium. We're in the Business District now. Victoria Street is one long stretch of smart lounge-bars, plus some lovely pubs to rest those tired feet over a slow drink.

Between here and the Shopping Centre is Mathew Street, mad at weekends. It's a short walk to Queen Square, more of a foodie destination but with Yates's and The Rat & Parrot facing each other across the bus lane like two bookends of bacchanalia. On to the Cultural Quarter and up Lime Street for some classic gin palaces.

Rope Walks rocks. Concert Square throbs with jeans-and T-shirt bars and nearby Slater Street is Soho with a Scouse twist.

Up the hill, the Hope Quarter will bring out the bohemian in you. Student, stage-manager or secretary, you'll get that Greenwich Village feeling as the sun goes down – and often see famous faces fresh from performing at the Phil.

The following is just a sample, No space to mention the speed-dating, sports bars, Scouse House and hip-hop scene – you'll have to check the posters and flyers (KooKoo, Lemon Lounge, Chibuku, Circus etc) as you sally forth.

141 Bars and clubs

Pier Head and Albert Dock

Yeah, Baby...

Baby Cream
**Atlantic Pavilion,
Albert Dock L3 4AE**
Tel: **(0151) 707 1004**
Visit: **babycream.co.uk**
From the people that gave us global clubbing brand Cream and legendary Liverpool lounge Blue. The two best nights are Thursday, when alternative dance collective Ladytron play everything from Nancy Sinatra to The Fall, and Sunday, when Suncream's ambient sounds kick in. If you like the tracks, you can burn them onto a CD there and then – courtesy of the Creamselector touch-screen digital music dispenser. What will they think of next?

Baltic Fleet
33A Wapping L1 8DQ
Tel: **(0151) 709 3116**
Talk about a contrast. This is your traditional (and very tourist-friendly) dockside alehouse, with authentic nautical memorabilia and the kind of bevvies that put hair on a stevedore's wellies. A quick one, just to settle the dust...

Blue Bar & Grill
**Edwards Pavilion,
Albert Dock L3 4AF**
Tel: **(0151) 709 7097**
Visit: **lyceumgroup.co.uk/bluebar**
For Blue, read bling. Lots of it. The deejay session du jour is Sunday's Babylicious in Baby Blue, the private members lounge. Just tell them you know Felix Da Housecat.

Pan American Club
**Britannia Pavilion,
Albert Dock L3 4AD**
Tel: **(0151) 702 5849**
Visit: **lyceumgroup.co.uk/panamerican**
Gwyneth Paltrow tippled in this immaculate sanctum recently (probably not a brown-over-mild) when hubbie Chris Martin was recording with Coldplay at Parr Street (see 3345 on page 149).

Platinum Lounge powder rooms

Garlands girls

Business District

Anderson's Bar
26 Exchange Street East L2 3PH
Tel: **(0151) 243 1330**
One-time piano bar at lower-ground level that was re-furbed and reopened at the end of 2002. Very busy at lunchtimes and a favourite with post-work professionals.

Garlands
8-10 Eberle Street L2 2AG
Tel: **(0151) 236 3307**
The Love Parade, Mardi Gras and Rio Carnival rolled into one super-kitsch disco. Men in tutus, this way please...

Late Lounge
3 Victoria Street L2 5QA
Tel: **(0151) 236 4832**
Between Metro and The Marquee, a big and beautiful lounge with pumping Scouse House on Sunday.

Living Room
15 Victoria Street
Tel: **(0151) 236 1999**
Visit: **livingroom.co.uk**
Arguably the classiest honky-tonk in town – dig that grand piano – and the brainchild of Tim Bacon, MD of Living Ventures, whose vision was to create "an environment that caters for a broad mix of people, I love the idea of a place for everyone." Result: a cool, airy interior with colonial browns and creams and 150 cocktails.

Ma Boyle's
Tower Gardens,
Tower Buildings L3 1AB
Tel: **(0151) 236 1717**
Cosy downstairs gem at the back of the redeveloped Tower Buildings. Cracking seafood platters, great maritime copper murals.

Best of 3...
gay venues

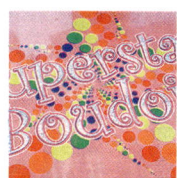

■ **Superstar Boudoir,** Stanley Street. The busiest and trendiest gay bar in town, with singers, drag acts and 1,000 customers from all over the North West at weekends.

■ **The Lisbon,** Stanley Street. On the corner with Victoria Street, and there before Liverpool's gay village was a gay village.

■ **The Navy,** Stanley Street. Port of call before heading to pumping bar and club Addiction and Masquerade around the corner.

Bars and clubs

This is the Newz

Marquee
9 Fowler Buildings,
Victoria Street L2
Tel: (0151) 227 2127
Visit: marqueeukltd.co.uk
Lounge bar and restaurant run by a Lebanese lecturer and Jordanian-Palestinian accountant, old friends in Liverpool for 20 years. Also starring a Syrian chef and solid RnB night on Sunday, brought to you by local radio deejay and London exile, Spykatcha.

Metro Eating Room & Bar
5-9 Fowlers Building, Victoria Street L2 5QA
Tel: (0151) 236 2200
Just turned two in summer 2004, a lounge venue with a saloon-type bar and exposed-brick interior reminiscent of all those dockside warehouses.

Newz Bar
New Zealand House,
18 Water Street L2 0TD
Tel: (0151) 236 2025
Visit: newzbrasserie.com
One of the joints in which to be seen, so get glammed up and prepare to queue at weekends. Suit sans neckwear for the gentlemen, little black dresses for the ladies.

Pacific Bar & Grill
Pacific Chambers,
11 Temple Street L2 5RH
Tel: (0151) 236 0270
Visit: pacificbarandgrill.com
Multi TV screens behind the bar, a great selection of champagne and lots of little corners to lounge and linger – not least the VIP Red Room – housed in one of the Business District's most charming neo-classical buildings.

Pig & Whistle
Covent Garden L2 8UA
Tel: **(0151) 236 4760**
Historic spit 'n' sawdust tavern by the Racquet Club and Thistle Hotel. 'Emigrants supplied' is still visible on an ancient brass plate.

The Place
38-40 Victoria Street L1 6BX
Tel: **(0151) 255 1252**
Opened by ex-Liverpool footballer John Aldridge, with an Asian Fusion restaurant called Thyme upstairs.

Platinum Lounge
1 Beetham Plaza, 25 Strand L2 0XW
Tel: **(0151) 227 9501**
Visit: **platinumlounge.co.uk**
Swanky without looking smug, it bills itself as an 'ambience of luxury in a first-class environment'. Low ceilings, grid lighting and glass-doored, unisex toilets. Make mine a Martini and Monte Cristo.

Rigby's
23-25 Dale Street L2 2EZ
Tel: **(0151) 236 3269**
It was founded in 1726. It used to be called The George. It's got a back-room that recalls the low-beamed ceiling of a ship. And it's packed with Horatio Nelson memorabilia. Admiral stuff.

Ship & Mitre
133 Dale Street
Tel: **(0151) 236 0859**
Visit: **shipandmitre.co.uk**
Like your cask-conditioned ales? Love this superb freehouse. Art Deco exterior, and inside deliveries every week from Germany, Belgium and the Czech Republic – often just one barrel of a particular brew.

The White stuff

White Bar @ Radisson SAS
105 Old Hall Street L3 9BS
Tel: **(0151) 966 1500**
Visit: **radisson.com**
Plush watering-hole at posh new hotel. They've kept the original fisherman's cottages on the outside and concocted some adorable Martinis behind the bar. The kind of place where George Benson could have a nice chat with Alexander McQueen while Posh and Becks listened in around the white piano.

Ye Cracke
13 Rice Street L1 7BN
Tel: **(0151) 709 4171**
A haunt of art-school student John Lennon – in June 1960 he formed his first band, The Dissenters, over a pint in these premises. Unspoilt with a stained-glass window and a snug called The War Office named after patrons who gathered here to discuss the Boer War.

Bars and clubs

Shopping Centre

**Best of 3...
Irish bars**

■ **Flanaghan's Apple,** Mathew Street. Beatleville boozer icing the Black Stuff with shamrocks long before the designer Paddy pubs arrived.

■ **The Liffey,** Renshaw Street. The waters of which 'made Guinness famous all over the world'.

■ **McHale's Irish American Bar,** Lime Street. The only Liver Bird with a shamrock in its beak. And a little mention for TP Molly's on Victoria Street. Which makes four Irish bars. So there.

■ **Dr Duncan's**
St John's House,
St John's Lane L1 1HF
Tel: **(0151) 709 5100**
Visit: **cainsbeer.com/pubs/doctorduncans.html**
By Queen Square and named after Liverpool's first Medical Officer of Health, who took on cholera and grim Victorian housing conditions and won (there's a great biog of him on the website). Count your blessings as you sup slowly in the ornate tiled surroundings.

■ **The Grapes**
25 Mathew Street L2 6RE
Tel: **(0151) 236 2961**
See that little table in the corner over there? That's where the Beatles used to sit for a pre-Cavern pint, that is. See that photograph on the wall? That's them actually doing it. Hang on, someone's getting their guitar out...

■ **Montreal**
56-58 Stanley Street L2
So new, we can't even give you the full postcode or phone number, and the next big thing in 'style socialising'. This is a seven-storey converted building with luxury lofts upstairs, a separate bar and restaurant, private members lounge and night club. The brainchild of the entrepreneurs behind Ronnie Scott's in London, and aiming for 'an eclectic but harmonious clientele'. Yowzer.

■ **The White Star**
4 Rainford Gardens L2 6PT
Tel: **(0151) 231 6861**
Teeny-weeny pub just off Mathew Street and plastered with shipping ephemera (White Star was one of Liverpool's pre-eminent ocean-going lines). Get there early on a Friday night or it's standing-room only on deck.

Cultural Quarter

■ **The Dispensary**
87 Renshaw Street L1 2SP
Tel: **(0151) 709 2160**
Visit: **cainsbeer.com/pubs/thedispensary1.html**
One of the original Cains brewery pubs, restored as a traditional Victorian alehouse with authentic pharmaceutical items and original fixtures and fittings from old chemist shops, and a good stop-off if you're heading up the hill into the Hope Quarter. Did we mention, by the way, that Cains are creating a special 2008 Ale to celebrate the big year?

■ **The Vines**
81 Lime Street L4 8SX
Tel: **(0151) 709 3977**
You can't miss its preposterous corner tower with a dome and obelisk. You shouldn't miss its superb baroque interior (that's a zodiac on the ceiling). Designed by Walter Aubrey Thomas, four years before he worked on the Royal Liver Building, for the brewer Robert Cain who wanted 'to so beautify the public houses under his control that they would be an ornament to the town of his birth'. Universally known as 'The Big House'.

Rope Walks

■ Baa Bar
43-45 Fleet Street L1 4AR
Tel: **(0151) 707 0610**
One of the city's original pre-club venues, the first real 'designer' conversion of a Liverpool industrial building into an entertainment venue (by developers Urban Splash back in 1991) and now one of the most successful brands in the North West. History footnote: outside the bar, the words 'rope', 'twine' and 'hessian' are still visible on an old, old façade.

■ Bar Fresa
11 Colquitt Street L1 4DE
Tel: **(0151) 706 0070**
While we're being historical, this late-night bar towards the top of Rope Walks is in the basement of the old Liverpool Royal Institution (built in 1815) dedicated to the promotion of literature, science and the arts, and before that the home and business premises of banker and city celebrity Thomas Parr, after whom the nearby street is named. Pay attention now, we'll be testing you later.

■ Beluga
40 Wood Street L1 4AQ
Tel: **(0151) 708 8896**
Smooth and sleek (just like a small white Arctic Ocean whale, in many ways), and a relaxed watering hole next door to Revolution. It was one of the first bars to initiate a females-first policy. In the middle of things, but a bit more chilled than its noisy neighbours.

Concert Square, when you're in the Mood

147 Bars and clubs

Bluu
Old Tea Factory Building, St Peter's Square, Fleet Street L1 4AS
Tel: **(0151) 709 8462**
The first Bluu was born in Hoxton, east London, so don't be surprised if you spot a lingering 'fin' among the punters. A place for conspicuous consumption, a dancefloor with a tropical-beach mural and a time-delay sound-system that subtly controls the volume of music in each room. Yup, this is what they thought of next.

Colin's Bridewell
Campbell Square L1 5BL
Tel: **(0151) 707 8003**
An old police station converted into a cool, airy bar with a restaurant upstairs. In 1860 Charles Dickens, on one of his many visits to Liverpool, was sworn-in here as an honorary constable. And that's not just the booze talking.

The Jacaranda
23 Slater Street
Tel: **(0151) 707 8281**
A few years ago they found murals by John Lennon behind the walls upstairs. The ground floor is a good place to quench your thirst after a Rope Walks walkabout.

Barfly @ The Masque
90 Seel Street L1 4BH
Tel: **(0151) 707 6171**
Visit: **masquevenue.fsnet.co.uk.**
A bar and club rolled into one streetwise shack, and the epicentre of Liverpool's urban music scene. Cheeky, trashy, funky, and all facilitated by the tastiest young turntable technicians. (Another Charles Dickens footnote: he gave readings from his novels here when it was a theatre in the mid-1800s.)

Nation
Wolstenholme Square
Tel: **(0151) 709 1693**
One day there'll be Blue Badge guides outside this modest venue, telling crowds of tourists about the halcyon days of Cream. The global clubbing brand may have different peaks to conquer these days, but Nation still hosts Bugged Out! on Saturday and student night Medication on Wednesday.

Barfly on the wall

Prohibition
1A Bold Street L1 4DJ
Tel: **(0151) 707 2333**
Visit: **prohibition.uk.com**
You don't get many chances to use the word 'agog' in a book like this. But that'll be your expression when you see the spectacular domed ceiling and chandelier in this venue's restaurant (serving New American cuisine). The cocktail bar serves mad specialities (the Parisienne, for instance, is Martell cognac, grand marnier, pear puree and honey topped with cinnamon) and downstairs there's a modern-day 'speakeasy' called The Cotton Club with Sinatra tributes on Sunday. It's all in the Old Lyceum Club and brought to life by the team behind The Living Room on Victoria Street. Decadent? Certainly. Dirty? Depends where you're coming from.

Society
64 Duke Street L1 5AA
Tel: **(0151) 708 9088**
One of Liverpool's best-loved clubs, now resolutely re-established after moving from its old home on Fleet Street, and what you get when you cross 'mansion chic' with 'contemporary vogue'. They spent a cool £2million renovating this Grade II listed building, with a little decorative help from New York-based interior designer Lola Bordanski who took ideas from places like Las Vegas, Barcelona, London and Ibiza. The stunning fibre-optic chandelier inside sums up her ethos. As we write, 'Scent' is the big night on Friday. It'll help, as a rule, if you're fairly broad-minded.

Tea Factory
79-82 Wood Street L1 4DQ
Tel: **(0151) 708 7008**
Next door to FACT and another bar in which to see and be seen – they call it 'urban and contemporary but not too pretentious'. Offers 50 champagne cocktails, 30 carefully-sourced rums and 24 loose-leaf teas. Well, obviously.

Velvet Lounge
59 Bold Street L1 4EZ
Tel: **(0151) 709 0303**
Visit: **velvetlounge.info**
Talk about an appropriate name. An exclusive venue for Liverpool's lords and ladies, plus visiting aristocracy. The hot new night is Groove on Friday, with four deejays spinning the wheels of steel from 9pm till 3am. Under the luxurious floor is a members-only bar called Bottom Drawer.

Vue Bar & Grill
2 Campbell Square L1 5AX
Tel: **(0151) 709 6965**
Lounge lizardry opposite Colin's Bridewell, with an informal terraced café bar. A great place to hang out on a summer's evening.

3345
Parr Street L1 4JN
Tel: **(0151) 708 6345**
Visit: **3345parrst.com**
Ooh, isn't that a pop star? Probably. This 'social oasis designed for creatives in the heart of the city centre' is part of the famous recording studio complex. If you ask nicely, they might let you play with some cymbals. Better off just chilling in the perfect retreat when Rope Walks is rocking.

Best of 3...
student hang-outs

■ **Krazy House,** Wood Street. Alt Rock and loud, blaring metal if you're that way inclined. Bills itself as 'the biggest student venue in the North West'.

■ **Heebie Jeebies,** Seel Street. Subterranean venue with three bars, lounge-style booth seating and, of course, lots of bar promotions.

■ **Café La'go,** Seel Street. A wind-assisted NUS card away from the Tea Factory, with Motown, 60s soul and frequent Sunday acoustic sessions.

Hope Quarter

Best of 3... party venues

Royal Daffodil. Cruising Mersey ferry with two saloons, a top sound system and room for over 250 revellers (0151 330 1458).

Palm House. Up to 400 people can party beneath the majestic glass canopy of Sefton Park's Grade II listed wonder (0151 726 9304).

City Exchange Atrium. A glass palace in the Post & Echo building (Business District) with an open-plan mezzanine (0151 472 2805).

Blackburn Arms
24 Catharine Street L8 7NL
Tel: (0151) 708 0252
A congenial establishment in which to feel at ease discussing Calasso's treatise on the origins of Western self-consciousness, or Carragher's propensity to blow snot through his nostril when he's knackered.

The Casa
29 Hope Street L1 9BQ
Tel: (0151) 709 2148
Small-but-perfectly-formed bar that also functions as a creative arts outlet for the dockers community in the city and has a great-value bistro-café downstairs. A former writer in residence here was Nicholas Allt, author of just-published The Boys from The Mersey (see page 208).

The Magnet
39-45 Hardman Street L1 9AS
Tel: (0151) 709 6969
Aptly-named – it draws punters like moths to a flame from Thursday onwards A packed bar upstairs and pre-meditated mayhem in the labyrinthine basement. You should try it. We think you'll like it.

Peter Kavanagh's
2-6 Little Egerton Street L8 7LY
Tel: (0151) 709 3443
Much-loved public house that reached the grand old age of 100 not out in 1997, and it's got the Victorian décor to prove it. It was named after a charismatic local designer – those are his tables in the snug – and adorned with murals of scenes from Dickens and Hogarth.

The Philharmonic Hotel
36 Hope Street L1 9BX
Tel: (0151) 707 2837
So good we've mentioned it twice (see page 92). Proper name, the Philharmonic Dining Rooms. Just say the Phil – everyone'll know where you mean. World famous, and what a place to meet as a starting-point for the evening.

The Pilgrim
34 Pilgrim Street L1 9HB
Tel: (0151) 709 2302
You go downstairs. You see lots of LIPA students and Beatles pictures on the walls. You say hello to Joe, the hospitable proprietor. You have a pint or three. You break into something from the White Album. You draw a tremendous burst of silence. You did your best and that's all that counts.

The Residents Lounge
**Hope Street Hotel,
40 Hope Street L1 9DA**
Tel: (0151) 709 3000
Underneath the restaurant and boutique hotel, into a chilled environment with live music on Friday nights and beautiful people everywhere you look. Chin chin.

Roscoe Head
24-26 Roscoe Street L1 2SX
Tel: (0151) 709 4365
Only 21 pubs in Britain have featured in every copy of the CAMRA Good Beer Guide since 1974. You're propping up the bar in one of them. It's only diddy, but who said size matters? Named after one of Liverpool's philanthropists, many of whose possessions are displayed over in Central Library.

Bars and clubs

What's to do...

■ The Juice FM listener knows how to party. Big time. Living for the weekend is something other people do, because when you've got Monday, Tuesday, Wednesday and Thursday, who can be bothered waiting until Friday? Without a doubt Liverpool is the most happening city in the country. Everywhere you look, there are new bars and clubs springing up. And the typical Liverpool clubber totally makes the effort, it's just second nature to them.

One of the things that we at Juice are proud of is that our presenter line-up comes from Liverpool. This means that they know what they're talking about on air. They don't stay in watching the TV every night, that's for certain. Not that the words 'opening' and 'envelope' spring to mind. Plus, come the weekend, Juice broadcasts live from three city-centre clubs. So even if you're staying in, you can still be out!

151 **Advertorial**

- A la carte restaurant
- Monthly menus
- Lounge Bar menu
- Open from midday to midnight 7 days
- Cocktail Lounge bar with a relaxing chilled out atmosphere
- Outside Piazza with seating for 80 till 10pm
- Breakfast business meetings with Plasma for presentations
- Available for private hire

VUE BAR & GRILL
VICTORIA SQUARE > LUGSDALE ROAD > WIDNES > WA8 6DJ T> 0151 257 8811 F> 0151 420 9084
2 > CAMPBELL SQUARE > LIVERPOOL > L1 5AX T> 0151 709 6965 F> 0151 709 6948
WWW.VUEBAR.COM   Company Registration No. 5005990

In association with:

Big spenders

Haute couture or urbanwear? Whatever your passion in fashion, you'll find it here. Let's shop...

■ How can you tell that you're shopping in Liverpool? The streets are packed, there's a lavish helping of style and fashion stores, and somewhere a lonesome trumpeter is playing From Russia With Love.

Albert Dock has some fabulous furnishings and homeware shops, but the main drag is Church Street with the Cavern Walks and Clayton Square (now with its 'Big Screen') malls at either end.

All the big department and chain stores are present (Body Shop, Boots, Burtons, Dorothy Perkins, Gap, HMV, John Lewis, Karen Millen, Littlewoods, Marks and Spencer, Next, Top Shop, Virgin Megastore, WH Smith). But it's the unique boutiques and independents that'll really float your boat, becoming more quirky the further you venture up Bold Street (where the Shopping Centre blends into Rope Walks).

With the Met Centre (Armani and Flannels) opening on Whitechapel (near Mathew Street) and a multi-million-pound retail arcadia set for Paradise Street, shoppers are only going to be spoilt for more choice over the next few years. Goodness, how on earth will we all cope?

Shops

Location key:

PH Pier Head/Albert Dock
BD Business District
SC Shopping Centre
CQ Cultural Quarter
RW Rope Walks
HQ Hope Quarter

Shops 154

A warm welcome from Ms Westwood

Fashion

■ **Vivienne Westwood** SC
8 Mathew Street L2 6RE
Tel: **(0151) 227 2700**
Visit: **hervia.com**

"I offer a choice," says Vivienne Westwood. "My clothes are not about being a consumer. They're about being an individual. They're original, different, you've never seen them before. There isn't much choice in this world, and it is a real choice that I offer people."

Brilliantly creative, defiantly unpredictable and ever so slightly anarchic – you could say that Westwood and Liverpool were made for each other. Appropriately the grand dame of avant-garde has set up shop in Mathew Street, where the world has been shaken once before. →

155 | Shops

She's the first international designer to open a flagship, stand-alone store in the city, with all of her lines – for men and women – housed in the Cavern Walks boutique. That means the fabulous Gold Label, Red Label, Man and Anglomania, plus shoes, bags, sunglasses, jewellery, perfume and eyewear.

Once described as 'the Alice in Wonderland of the fashion world', Westwood has consistently defied contemporary fashion to design clothes that have defined eras – starting with the King's Road boutique she ran with Malcolm McLaren in the 1970s. She was the first British designer since Mary Quant to show in Paris. She paraded her collection in Tokyo as one of the top five designers in the world. And now she's gracing the 2008 European Capital of Culture with a brand that fits perfectly within Liverpool's exciting environment. Like a hand, perhaps, in a particularly elegant glove.

Westwood. Where else?

They're either giant perfume bottles or Kylie's left her boots behind

■ Cricket **SC**
**Cavern Walks,
Mathew Street L2 6RE**
Tel: **(0151) 207 4645**
Everyone who's anyone shops here. A beautifully laid-out boutique with an extra 3,000sq ft added in 2003 (and designed to replicate a catwalk), it stocks all those Stella, Roland Mouret, Pucci and Missoni must-haves you've been promising yourself.

■ Designer City **BD**
14-16 Victoria Street L2 6QE
Tel: **(0151) 236 9115**
Five years old and going strong for this celebrated designer-label shop that now has its first women's collection featuring Sportmax, Sonia Rykiel, Amanda Wakeley, Prada Sport, Missoni Sport, Versace Sport, Armani Jeans...

■ Drome for Men **SC**
46 Bold Street L1 4DS
Tel: **(0151) 709 1441**
Cutting-edge and imaginative menswear and accessories from the only Liverpool store mentioned in Caryn Franklin's Fashion UK directory. Stussy hats and bags, Maharishi designer toys, Vestal watches, Evisu gift boxes etc.

■ Drome Couture/Women **SC**
Cavern Walks L2 6RE
Tel: **(0151) 255 0525/1565**
Couture (the upstairs bit) was recently reviewed by the Sunday Times as 'styled like a New York gallery' and includes Dolce & Gabbanna, Cavalli, Gharani Strok, Betsey Johnson and Pringle Gold Label among its collections.

It just is Cricket

Shops

Loki? Corset is...

Women has funky stuff from Michiko Koshino, Guess, Miss Sixty, Diesel, Paul Frank and Stussy. Lots of awards, no surprises.

■ Giancarlo Ricci SC
45 Bold Street L1 4AL
Tel: **(0151) 708 8044**
Male and female fashion, from Armani to Versace, in this popular boutique near Karen Millen.

■ Jeff's SC
80 Bold Street L1 4HR
Tel: **(0151) 707 0880**
Visit: **jeffsofboldst.co.uk**
One of the city's leading independent stores and affectionately known as the Harrods of Liverpool. Three floors of ladies fashion, a personal-dresser service, Victorian tea-room and 250-year-old wishing well. What more could you ask for?

■ Lacoste SC
18 Whitechapel L1 6DS
Tel: **(0151) 227 2214**
Actually Wade Smith's Lacoste Boutique. The French label decamped here in March 2004 with a new, curved-white-wall concept for its store interior, the result of a collaboration between Paris-based architect Patrick Rubin and interior designer Christophe Pillet. It's their largest store in the UK.

■ Loki SC
Cavern Walks L2 6SE
Tel: **(0151) 255 1881**
Corset tops to die for, or at least gasp. Loki's designs have been used by national newspapers and described as 'garments for women who ooze femininity'.

Still need directions?

■ Open SC
54 Church Street L1 3AY
Tel: **(0151) 708 3322**
Through the arched entrance and into a cornucopia of designer clothing and concessions slap-bang in the middle of Church Street. Look out for Italian brand Belstaff's motorcycling goodies, and how about that limited-edition Che Guevara replica jacket as worn by Cameron Diaz?

■ Reiss SC
46-48 Stanley Street L1 6AL
Tel: **(0151) 227 9157**
Visit: **reiss.co.uk**
Just over the road from Wade Smith, a world of oak staircases, sandblasted walls and steel rafters. Oh, and award-winning, tailor-made clothes for style-conscious men and women.

■ Script HQ
75-77 Lime Street L1 1JQ
Tel: **(0151) 709 1900**
Glad rags for male gadabouts. Prada's the big seller, also Boss, Armani, Dolce & Gabbana, Versace.

■ Sidewalk RW
Petticoat Lane Arcade, 102 Bold Street L1 4HY
Tel: **(0151) 708 9697**
Menswear store stocking Armani, Prada, Versace, Lacoste and Boss.

■ Wade Smith SC
Mathew Street L2 6RE
Tel: **(0151) 255 1077**
Ultra-successful store synonymous with the city's style. Four floors of high fashion frequented by famous names, it was founded by David Wade-Smith, now director of the funky Room Store on Albert Dock.

Best of 3... record shops

■ **3 Beat,** Slater Street. At the forefront of worldwide house music for 10 years and now showcasing fresh new label talent. An honorable mention for nearby Bold Street Records, too.

■ **Probe,** Wood Street. Original and still the best, glam queen Pete Burns' old vinyl emporium is now opposite Liverpool Palace.

■ **XFade Records,** Dale Street. Imports, down-tempo, Detroit house, techno, garage, drum and bass etc...

Shops

All dressed up

Why Liverpool starts the trends and never follows the herd...

Lady in red

■ Around autumn 2002, mumurings of 'Livercool' began appearing in the news. Kira Joliffe, editor of style mag Cheapdate, said Scousers had "a great sense of fashion, they make so much effort and look so perfect." The superlatives gathered pace six months later when Isabella Blow, champion of new talent and fashion director of Tatler, ran a photo-shoot in the city and declared it "a place where tradition meets cutting-edge."

Liverpudlians always have had their own cute sense of style. Trendsetters rather than followers, they don't heed national notions of what's in or out, new or old, but do their own thing with a swagger. They were among the first in the UK to wear denim, brought in by sailors from America after the Second World War, and the Merseybeat scene had its own code of sharp dress. When the rest of the country embraced punk, Liverpool's youth went electronic and adopted a softer look.

This was the era of a club called Eric's. Pete Burns was flogging Westwood out of the back of Probe, Julian Cope was starting a flying-jacket trend all by himself, and in 1984 Frankie Goes To Hollywood launched the must-have garment of the year with a take on Katharine Hamnett's famous 'Ban Nuclear Weapons Now' T-shirt. Every wannabe fashionista wore one bearing the legend 'Frankie Says Relax Don't Do It'.

Liverpudlians also invented terrace fashion. 'Scallies' appeared in the late 70s (the south responded with 'casuals'), Liverpool FC fans with wedge haircuts and foreign sports labels acquired while watching their team in Europe. When the look caught on, they moved on. They wore semi-flares in the mid-80s and by the time it took hold nationwide they'd adopted the 'country gent' look of Barbours and tweed. Tracksuits came next and have remained an idiosyncrasy of Scouse street style ever since. Worn with the bottoms tucked into socks, and always Lacoste.

Shops

There's no one Liverpool look, but there is a collective desire to dress up – from the teengirl sub-culture of pyjamas to full-on glamour in the city's bars personified on Grand National Ladies Day when the best-dressed punter drives home in a new Jag.

Contrast is key and it shows in the plethora of shops. Wade Smith is the original designer boutique and forerunner to Cricket and Drome. Now comes Vivienne Westwood, whose canon 'Dress up more than down because then you'll have a great time' could've been written for the city. Store manager Jonathan Weir adds, "Liverpool is a good-looking city and this is mirrored by the people who love to dress up and dress well. The women are adventurous and have their own direction. And that sums up Westwood."

Vintage may be a byword now, but it's had a following in Liverpool for decades. 69A (Renshaw Street) has been established for 20 years, while Bulletproof (Hardman Street) sells its 60s and 70s clothes by weight. With retro concessions, a flea market and local designers, Quiggins on School Lane has been a Liverpool institution. Up on Slater Street is Liverpool Palace, three floors of independent outlets selling retro clothes and urbanwear.

Liverpudlians aren't just wearing it, they're designing it. Paula McCullock, under her label Prudence Wildeblood, showed her collection at London Fashion Week. Jason Ansell saw his first collection snapped up by Wade Smith. The Felix Blow Partnership has built up a loyal following for its 8703 brand. And an exhibition by JMU's fashion students, won rave reviews – a sure sign the future is bright.

That's never been in doubt. After his magazine's photoshoot, Tatler editor Geordie Greig stated, "This is a super-sexy place, soon the whole world will catch on that Liverpool is having another renaissance." True, maybe, for fashion followers. But for Liverpudlians it's definitely a case of business as usual.

Woman in black

161 | Shops

Jewellery and accessories

On the rocks..

■ As a rule the whiter and clearer a diamond, the better. A good diamond should be at least the colour of a gin and tonic, but it'll usually have some sort of cloud, feather or crystal-shaped 'inclusion' which is its unique, natural hallmark. The 'cut' should be even, regular and light-reflecting to release fire and brilliance through its facets – tiny planes that create angles to reflect and disperse light through the top of the stone. 'Carat' refers to the size of the diamond. One carat is divided into 100 points, so a diamond weighing 50 points is half-a-carat. But two diamonds of equal size can have very different values depending on their colour and cut

■ **The Bead Shop** **SC**
58 Whitechapel L1 6EG
Tel: **(0151) 709 7858**
Now based by Queen Square after a long spell in the alternative arcade Quiggins. Does exactly what it says above the door.

■ **Boodle & Dunthorne** **BD**
Boodles House, Lord Street L2 9SQ
Tel: **(0151) 227 2525**
Visit: **boodleanddunthorne.com**
A Liverpool institution and true destination shop. The new interior and glass staircase is the work of Eva Jiricna, who also designed the the new foyer for Selfridges on Oxford Street. The stones are sourced by Nicholas Wainwright, one of Britain's gemmologists. And the pieces are designed to stand the test of time and reflect the nuances of haute couture. Boodles call it, simply, 'jewellery in fashion'.

■ **David M Robinson** **SC**
24 Church Alley L1 3DD
Tel: **(0151) 236 2720**
Visit: **davidmrobinson.co.uk**
A quick history lesson. Stonier's was a Liverpool firm, founded in 1861, that supplied 50,000 items of bone china to the Titanic, including the distinctive cobalt-blue First Class dinner plates. At one point the company was sold to Stuart Crystal of Edinburgh, but Liverpool's David M Robinson bought (and brought) it back – and today Stonier's stocks Lladro's finest Valencian porcelain and Swarovski crystals, plus giftware by Versace, Villeroy and Boch, Kosta Boda, Wedgewood, Waterford (and special designs by John Rocha and Jasper Morrison). Don't you just love a happy ending?

■ **Pykes the Jewellers** **SC**
24-26 Whitechapel L1 6DZ
Tel: **(0151) 708 8588**
Silversmiths and watchmakers, too. Founded 125 years ago and now with prestigious new headquarters in Whitechapel, diamonds personally sourced from Antwerp and top European brands like Fabergé, Links of London and Pianegonda.

■ **Silverbergs** **SC**
40 Whitechapel L1 6DZ
Tel: **(0151) 709 2012**
Premier stockists of the most sensational shades in town. Here – and only here – you'll find Armani snakeskin leather sunglasses, and limited-edition, Swarovski diamond-encrusted shades by Dior (in silver, black or red).

■ **Wongs** **SC**
5 Rainford Square L2 6PX
Tel: **(0151) 227 1677**
Family business with a workshop on the premises that specialises in platinum jewellery, stronger, rarer

Finding something special

A few delightful destination shops to tell you about...

■ Let's start with homeware and interiors, specifically two venues on Albert Dock and three at the top of Bold Street. Down by the riverside, Ocean (0151 707 3763), the contemporary furniture and accessories experts, are based in Richard and Judy's old den. Next door, The Room Store (708 0000) is a one-stop shop for designer furniture, kitchenware, bathroom products and lighting. Alessi, B&B Italia, Gandia Blasco, Flos, Kartell and Vitra, you'll find it all here, plus timeless classics by Ron Arad, Achille Castiglioni, Charles and Ray Eames, Eileen Gray and Ludwig Mies van der Rohe. Two relaxing floors to browse, have a coffee then come back and splash out (in the shop, not the water).

Up in Rope Walks there's oriental inspiration at Zen Interiors (0151 707 7700) – dig those groovy monkeys outside – and The Lotus Room (0151 709 8009), stockists of the finest hand-crafted Balinese furniture and giftware, and curators of a gallery for local artists. Across Bold Street is Utility (707 9919), the city's only Conran stockists. We're particularly enamoured with his elliptically curvaceous Love sofa and Chaperon seat, but then again we like the iconic Bombo bar stools, too. You, on the other hand, may fall for the fabulous handmade jewellery, ceramic, glass and wood gifts at the Bluecoat Display Centre (0151 236 1282) on School Lane, or the Art Deco antiques at Circa 1900 (0151 236 1282) in Water Street's India Buildings (the Burlington Arcade of the north, we'll have you know).

Want something a little more modern? For the very latest in audio and technology, seek out Bang & Olufsen (0151 236 3000) on Castle Street (their tiny BeoSound 2 MP3 player is a best-seller) and Sevenoaks Sound & Vision (0151 707 8417) on Lord Street with super-slim plasma screens-amundo. Phew.

All the fun

■ As well as the indoor St John's Centre (off Church Street with an excellent food counter) and thrice-yearly Lord Street European Market (everything from pumpkin bread to pine-tree honey), there's a Heritage Market every Sunday at Stanley Dock (north of Pier Head) with 500 independent stalls. Great Homer Street Market (north-east) attracts 3,000 shoppers every Saturday, and there's a Farmers Market at Chavasse Park (Pier Head) every third Saturday of the month. Antiques experts should head for the Collectables Fair at St George's Hall in the first week of every month, with up to 130 sellers specialising in Art Deco.

163 **Shops**

NHS Walk-in Centres

Are you an early bird?

NHS Walk-in Centre are open early in the morning, offering a wide range of services, treatments and consultations with experienced NHS nurses.

no appointment necessary
Open early 'til late, seven days a week

Liverpool (City) NHS Walk-in Centre, 4 Charlotte Row, Great Charlotte Street, Liverpool L1 1HU
Crystal Close (off Oswald Street) L13 2GA Telephone: 0151 285 3565

OPEN WEEKDAYS 7am - 10pm OPEN WEEKENDS/BANK HOLIDAY 9am - 10pm

NHS Walk-in Centres

Are you a night owl?

no appointment necessary

NHS walk-in centres are open late in the evening, offering a wide range of services, treatments and consultations with experienced NHS nurses.

Liverpool (City) NHS Walk-in Centre, 4 Charlotte Row, Great Charlotte Street, Liverpool L1 1HU
Crystal Close (off Oswald Street) L13 2GA Telephone: 0151 285 3565

OPEN WEEKDAYS 7am - 10pm OPEN WEEKENDS/BANK HOLIDAY 9am - 10pm

In association with:

NATIONAL MUSEUMS LIVERPOOL

Where the art is

Presenting a munificence of museums and galleries...

In December 2003, Sir Jeremy Isaacs gave a speech at FACT. The former director general of the Royal Opera House was also chairman of the judging panel that, six months earlier, had chosen Liverpool as European Capital of Culture for 2008. "Without question," he told a full house, "this city has the greatest single conglomeration of galleries and museums of any city outside London – and that is a very strong calling card indeed." Shall we see what he means?

Arts and culture

National Museums Liverpool

He's Henry VIII, he is

■ **National Museums Liverpool**
Tel: (0151) 207 0001
Visit: liverpoolmuseums.org.uk
This is the collective name for the eight museums and galleries that make up the greatest collection of artefacts, paintings, specimens and objects collectively held under single ownership in the country. They are: the Conservation Centre, Lady Lever Art Gallery, Liverpool Museum, Merseyside Maritime Museum and HM Customs & Excise National Museum, Museum of Liverpool Life, Sudley House and the Walker Art Gallery.

In February 2004, NML was awarded the Freedom of Liverpool, and in 2008 all of its venues will be open for 24 hours to celebrate Die Lange Nacht on midsummer's night, the longest night of the year. As it is, they're open Monday to Saturday 10am-5pm, Sunday 12-5pm unless stated, and entrance to all exhibitions and events is free.

■ **Conservation Centre** SC
Whitechapel L1 6HZ
Tel: (0151) 478 4999
Visit: conservationcentre.org.uk
Awards galore for the UK's first national conservation centre, housed in a Victorian goods office. The statue in the foyer is the original 'Liverpool' from the roof of the Walker, sculpted in Rome by John Warrington Wood in 1875. She's a seated woman surrounded by bales of cotton, a propeller and trident (to symbolise the city's maritime power), a palette with paint brushes and a set square (for her cultural aspirations), and she's carved from the same Carrara marble used by Michelangelo.

Location key:
PH Pier Head/Albert Dock
BD Business District
SC Shopping Centre
CQ Cultural Quarter
RW Rope Walks
HQ Hope Quarter

Arts and culture 166

Lady Lever Art Gallery
Port Sunlight Village CH62 5EQ
Tel: **(0151) 478 4136**
Over the water for the collected art treasures of Edwardian philanthropist and soap magnate, William Hesketh Lever. Summer 2004 saw an exhibition from two watercolour masters, JMW Turner and Daniel Alexander Williamson, fresh from a showing at Tate Britain. As well as paintings, the gallery has porcelain, tapestries and memorabilia relating to Lever's fascination with Napoleon.

JMW Turner: what Lever patrons come to expect

Liverpool Museum CQ
William Brown Street L3 8EN
Tel: **(0151) 478 4399**
One of the country's premier museums, featuring a dazzling new atrium, Natural History Centre and Planetarium, and attracting 4,000 visitors a day (and lots of school trips). There are Egyptian mummies, Greek and Roman artefacts and priceless collections from the Amazon Rainforest.

"Ah forget it, Narcissus lad, it was only 5p..."

Merseyside Maritime Museum and HM Customs and Excise National Museum PH
Albert Dock L3 4AQ
Tel: **(0151) 478 4499**
Telling the story of one of the world's greatest ports and the people who used it. Find out what it felt like to cross mighty oceans as an emigrant or a slave. Experience the palatial world of luxurious liners like the Titanic and Lusitania. And explore the astonishing history of smuggling since the 1700s. Four floors of permanent and new exhibitions reflecting Liverpool's seafaring heritage.

Landscape by Liverpool's David Alexander Williamson

167 Arts and culture

Ship's figurehead at the Museum of Liverpool Life

Arts and culture 168

Museum of Liverpool Life PH
Pier Head L3 1PZ
Tel: **(0151) 478 4080**
From a statue of Billy Fury, the country's first great rock 'n' roller, to authentic pieces of the old Spion Kop, this is the ultimate celebration of Liverpudlian culture.

Appropriately for 2004, the Year of Faith in One City, there are also fascinating religious objects like an early 19th Century Jewish miniature ark, Islamic prayer mats and Catholic rosary beads.

Sudley House
Mossley Hill Road, Aigburth L18 8BX
Tel: **(0151) 724 3245**
With masterpieces by Turner, Gainsborough and a host of Pre-Raphaelites housed in the former home of a wealthy Victorian ship-owner in Liverpool's leafy southern suburbs.

The Walker CQ
William Brown Street L3 8EL
Tel: **(0151) 478 4199**
The first British public art gallery and without doubt one of the finest in Europe. Where shall we start? The full-length Henry VIII portrait is based on the Whitehall mural by Hans Holbein destroyed by fire 300 years ago and is thought to have belonged his favourite wife Jane Seymour, while William Hogarth's 1745 painting of David Garrick as Richard III captures the Marlon Brando of his day in full method-acting mode.

John Brett's The Stonebreaker is the favourite painting of Sir Peter Blake (designer behind the Beatles Sgt Pepper album cover), who calls it "a tiny, jewel-like painting among a superb Pre-Raphaelite collection." And the Tinted Venus, whose flesh-coloured body, blue eyes and golden hair caused a scandal when she was shown in London in 1862, is the beloved creation of local neo-classical sculptor John Gibson. He studied in Rome like John Warrington Wood (see Conservation Centre) and was loathe to give her up, writing to the wife of the rich Liverpool patron who commissioned him: "It would be as difficult for me to part with her as it would be for your husband to part with you."

Have we mentioned the Rubens, Rembrandt, Seurat, Cezanne, Poussin, Degas, Freud, Hockney, Gilbert and George?

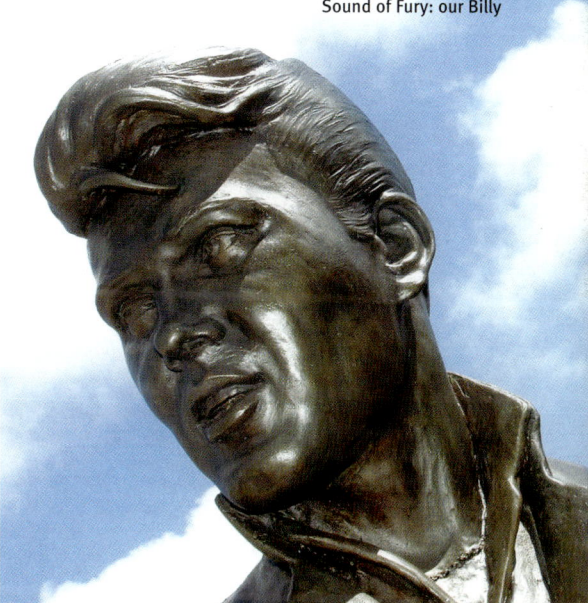

Sound of Fury: our Billy

Arts and culture

What's to do...

■ Oh Swallow Swallow is one of four works by Pre-Raphaelite artist John Strudwick at Sudley House, depicting an event from the poem The Princess by Tennyson in which a bird bears a message from the poet to his absent lover: 'Oh Swallow, flying from the golden woods, Fly to her, and pipe and woo her, and make her mine, And tell her, tell her, that I follow thee'. Over at The Walker, Edgar Degas imbues the most mundane of tasks with an ethereal beauty in Woman Ironing. He was labelled an Impressionist, but this late 19th-century painting rejects the plein-air subject matter of peers like Monet and Renoir and focuses on human movement. Just two of many marvels on display at the eight free venues of National Museums Liverpool.

Museums and galleries

■ Bluecoat Arts Centre/ Display Centre **SC**
School Lane L1 3BX
Tel: **(0151) 709 5297**
Visit: **bluecoatartscentre.com / bluecoatdisplaycentre.com**

The Grade I listed cornerstone of Liverpool's artistic life, and currently undergoing an exciting refurbishment of its studios, stages, workshops and galleries (but very much open to the public). With a continuous programme of innovative exhibitions and events, BAC has pioneered the visual and performing arts for decades. Just recently BDC was one of only six British galleries outside London represented at COLLECT at the V&A – the UK's first annual fair exclusively for contemporary applied decorative art.

Ceramics at Bluecoat

■ Central Library and Record Office **CQ**
William Brown Street L3 8EW
Tel: **(0151) 233 5835**

Its Picton Reading Room is a work of art in itself. Don't miss John James Audubon's magnificent Birds of America book and the equally rare volumes in the Hornby Library and Oak Room.

Eagles at Central Library

■ CUBE **RW**
82 Wood Street L1 4DQ
Visit: **cube.org.uk**

As in, Centre for the Understanding of the Built Environment. Near the Tea Factory in the raucous lower reaches of Rope Walks, in 2004 it secured the first UK exhibition of David Adjaye, who designed the Nobel Peace Centre in Oslo and the award-winning Social night clubin London's West End.

Red rooms at CUBE

Arts and culture

Best of 3...
Beatles art

■ **View II Gallery,**
Mathew Street.
Unconventional art like
Alex Corina's
marvellous 'Mona
Lennon' on tins cans,
tiles and dustbin lids.

■ **Mathew Street
Gallery.** Rare classics
like Robert Whittaker's
candid backstage
shots in Munich and
Abbey Road from the
mid-60s.

■ **Expresso Exchange,**
Victoria Street.
Artist Stephen Bowers'
excellent neo-
impressionist portraits
of the Fabs in the
early days.

■ **FACT RW**
88 Wood Street L1 4DQ
Tel: (0151) 707 4450
Visit: fact.co.uk
As in, Foundation for Arts and Creative Technology. The zinc-lined walls of Liverpool's 'arts project for the digital age' make an unforgettable first impression. Inside the £8.7million building, you'll find two galleries dedicated to new media artwork, and three state-of-the-art cinemas showing arthouse and mainstream movies. There's a dinky clubhouse for hire called The Box, plus cafés and bars with great views across the Liverpool cityscape. It's been called an unparalleled support system for UK artists and another icon of Liverpool's cultural and economic renaissance. We just think it's fab.

■ **Liverpool Academy of Arts RW**
36 Seel Street L45 7PA
Tel: (0151) 709 0735
Visit: la-art.co.uk
Dating back to 1763, the LAA is currently a small gallery dedicated to local artists, with an annual Beatles Art exhibition (last week in July to first in September).

■ **Open Eye Gallery RW**
28-32 Wood Street L1 4AQ
Tel: (0151) 709 9460
Visit: openeye.org.uk
Showcases innovative and challenging photography and media art with an international pedigree, including many world premieres and talks by the artists. From abstract and detached images of the modern world to the power of the veil in Islamic society.

It's a FACT

Arts and culture

Tate Liverpool **PH**
Albert Dock L3 4BB
Tel: **(0151) 702 7400**
Visit: **tate.org.uk/liverpool**
Otherwise known as the National Collection of Modern Art in the North of England. Around 600,000 visitors a year admire its works from the Tate Collection and special exhibitions of contemporary art, and past shows include Salvador Dali and Paul Nash. It's got a global reputation, and you'd be mad to miss it. Open Tuesday to Sunday 10am-5.50pm.

University of Liverpool Art Gallery **HQ**
6 Abercromby Square L69 7WY
Tel: **(0151) 794 2348**
Visit: **liv.ac.uk/artgall**
Works by Turner, Epstein and Freud, plus American wildlife artist JJ Aubudon, displayed in a beautiful Georgian terrace house.

View Two Gallery **SC**
23 Mathew Street L1 4LN
Tel: **(0151) 236 9555**
Three floors on Liverpool's Carnaby Street. Paintings, ceramics, jewellery and modern furniture. You'll fall for the prize-winning work of Anne Young, touted as the next Beryl Cook. Open Thursday to Saturday, 12-4pm.

Western Approaches Museum **BD**
1-3 Rumford Street L2 3SZ
Tel: **(0151) 227 2008**
A permanent reminder of Liverpool's crucial role as Area Command HQ for the Battle of the Atlantic. Eerie, underground, awe-inspiring.

Antony Gormley's Field, at Tate Liverpool in 2004

Art for everyone

Time raises Truth towards the light, on Ullet Road

In Ullet Road Unitarian Church, just off Sefton Park in south Liverpool, is a stained glass window (right) by the Pre-Raphaelite Sir Edwards Burne-Jones and William Morris, champion of the late 19th Century Arts & Crafts movement. Alongside are enigmatic murals (left) by Gerald Moira, the Portuguese symbolist who decorated one of London's most famous churches, All Saints.

Rich in statues and monuments from the Victorian era, Liverpool readily embraced later aesthetic movements. Its love for Art Nouveau in the early 1900s wasn't confined to the decor of the mighty liners anchored on the Mersey – the splendid gates of the Philharmonic Hotel (left, below) rival anything produced by Gaudi and the Modernists in Barcelona.

Art Deco, meanwhile, soared to sublime heights on the beautifully-sculptured facades of the Queensway tunnel entrances and ventilation shafts.

Among the best post-war public sculptures are Patrick Glyn Heesom's 'growing thresh of wings' outside the Litttlewoods Building on Old Hall Street, and the Piazza Waterfall at Beetham Plaza (both Business District), designed by Richard Huws to recreate the sound and fury of 'the restless, temperamental sea'.

More recent landmarks include The Great Escape, Edward Cronshaw's bronze sculpture of a man restraining a four-metre-high horse made of unravelling rope, and A Case History, John King's stack of luggage piled on Hope Street's pavement for the city's

Any resemblance to the lady on page 170 is probably intentional

Arts and culture

Crashing waves:
Piazza Waterfall

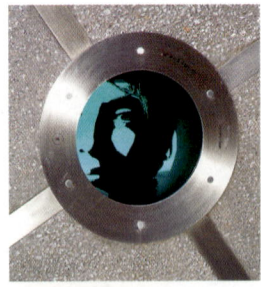

first Biennial in 1998. The same year, SuperLambBanana (right), by the Baltic Fleet pub on Wapping, was created by Japanese artist Taro Chiezo as a grotesque parody of genetic engineering.

Summer 2004 saw Penelope (below, right), the twisting, glowing steel sculpture by Cuban artist Jorge Pardo, make her grand entrance in Wolstenholme Square (Rope Walks) as a reference to both Liverpool's maritime past and the unshakable faith of Ulysses' wife in her husband's return after the Trojan War in the Greek myth.

Meanwhile the Faces of Liverpool (below, left) began to appear in blue glass portholes in the triangular garden at the foot of Beetham Tower (Business District), an urban art project celebrating the city's global connections, diverse culture and rich ethnic mix using simple geometry, symbols and maps. Among the contemporary residents featured are a man whose Japanese grandfather was Emperor Hirohito's cousin, a woman whose Russian grandparents were re-united with old friends after a chance meeting in Liverpool, and a man whose Yemeni father ran away to the city to get married.

We urge you to also view the murals of radical Liverpudlians by David Jacques running all along the walls of the Newz Bar (Water Street), the extensive private collection at the Racquet Club (Chapel Street), including a huge 19th Century copy of a medieval painting of the Medicis hunting, and Anthony Brown's wistful Waterfront in Hemingways café (Lower Duke Street).

Arts and culture 176

Strange fruit:
the yellow baa

177 Arts and culture

Performance

From beautiful ballet to sleazy urban sounds...

■ The finest opera and classical evenings at the Empire and Phil. The best of modern drama and dance at the Everyman and Playhouse, Neptune and Unity, and LIPA. And a dozen top comedy and gig venues. Let us entertain you. We insist.

Entertainment

River Mersey, Swan Lake, English National Ballet

Classical and musicals

■ **Liverpool Empire Theatre CQ**
Lime Street L1 1JE
Tel: (0151) 708 3200
Visit: liverpoolempire.co.uk
You know that feeling you get when you take your sit before an eagerly-anticipated performance in a beautiful theatre – all velvet seats, gilded décor, brocaded curtains and dizzyingly high ceiling – and a hush descends as the lights begin to dim? Double it and you've got the Empire. Only the Albert Hall can hold a candle to this stunning venue, recently refurbished and now just as grand with state-of-the-art facilities. In 2004 to date, it's staged the Nutcracker, Sleeping Beauty, Grease, Saturday Night Fever, Carmen, Turandot, The King & I and Blood Brothers, to name but a few. Whatever the show, at night there's a sensational view from the lounge bar across to St George's Hall and William Brown Street. Sublime.

■ **Liverpool Institute of Performing Arts HQ**
Mount Street L1 9HF
Tel: (0151) 709 4988
Visit: lipa.ac.uk
Tomorrow's stars today. LIPA runs two seasons of public productions (dance, drama and musicals) each year, in autumn and spring. Second and final-year students regularly perform in up to 30 shows in the Paul McCartney Auditorium and Sennheiser Studio Theatre – watch out for their evenings of show-stopping jazz. Early 2004 saw performances of Stephen Sondheim's Sunday in the Park and Peter Shaffer's Amadeus, among others.

■ **Philharmonic Hall HQ**
Hope Street L1 9BP
Tel: (0151) 709 3789
Visit: liverpoolphil.com
Home to the Royal Liverpool Philharmonic Orchestra – and so much more. There's a youth orchestra and gospel choir, and the hall regularly hosts gigs and world music concerts (from Bacharach to Buena Vista) plus audiences with intellectuals and raconteurs. Once you've admired the décor's riot of musical motifs, close your eyes and let some of the world's best musicians serenade you. Have we mentioned the movies yet? Classic Films at the Phil features everything from the Parisian splendour of Moulin Rouge to the hard-boiled noir of the Coen brothers, shown on the world's only surviving Walturdaw cinema screen. What's one of those? A screen with a proscenium that's raised through the stage via a system of antique counterweights That's what.

Beats EastEnders anyday

Entertainment

Drama and dance

■ **Everyman Theatre HQ**
Hope Street L1 9BH
Tel: (0151) 708 4776
Visit: everymanplayhouse.com
The Everyman and Playhouse (see below right) go together like, well, a pan of Scouse and a jar of pickled beetroot (i.e. very well indeed). Prolific and progressive for decades, they're now run as a single concern by Gemma Bodinetz and Deborah Aydon, artistic director and executive director respectively and a duo on a mission to restore Liverpool's reputation as a leading theatre destination. The Everyman has a reputation as a writer's theatre and just recently it's staged classics like The Merchant of Venice and new blockbusters like Dael Orlandersmith's Yellowman, one of the most acclaimed plays in the US. What we're trying to say is: if you're coming to Liverpool, you must-must-must visit this place.

Have your Phil

■ **Neptune Theatre SC**
Hanover Street L1 3DY
Tel: (0151) 709 7844
Visit: neptunetheatre.co.uk
A quirky, intimate venue famous for enticing some of the country's top comedy and musical acts. Great for family shows, too – recent performances include Beauty and the Beast, and Humpty Dumpty. Sunny side up, every time.

■ **The Playhouse SC**
Williamson Square L1 1EL
Tel: (0151) 709 4776
Visit: everymanplayhouse.com
Specialising in bold and creative interpretations of the very best drama. In 2004 it's put on a Noel Coward double-bill plus works by Bertold Brecht, Tom Stoppard, Brendan Behan and David Hare. This is, by the way, the oldest established repertory company n the country. So there.

■ **Unity Theatre HQ**
1 Hope Place L1 9BG
Tel: (0151) 709 4988
Visit: unitytheatreliverpool.co.uk
On the site of a synagogue and one of a select group of venues in the country formed before World War II 'to make theatres accessible to the great mass of the people'. It's maintained its reputation for staging innovative, adventurous work and regularly showcases rising talent from LIPA. There's children's theatre, too, plus a commitment to major city events (Writing on the Wall, Liverpool Comedy Festival and the Liverpool International Street Festival). Its patrons include actors Cathy Tyson, Ian Hart and Alison Steadman.

Blowing the trumpet for the Everyman and Playhouse

LIVERPOOL EVERYMAN AND PLAYHOUSE PRESENT

THEATRE MADE IN LIVERPOOL

THE AFFILIATED LIVERPOOL PLAYHOUSE
AND EVERYMAN THEATRES ARE CURRENTLY
ENJOYING A FRESH LEASE OF LIFE
INDEPENDENT ON SUNDAY

BOX OFFICE 0151 709 4776

Photography by Jon Barraclough

LIVERPOOL PLAYHOUSE BUILT IN 1866, HOUSED ENGLAND'S OLDEST REPERTORY COMPANY AND WAS RESPONSIBLE FOR LAUNCHING THE CAREERS OF SOME OF BRITAIN'S FINEST ACTORS AND WRITERS.

THE EVERYMAN FOUNDED IN 1964, QUICKLY BECAME A POWERFUL CREATIVE FORCE WITH A SIMILAR RECORD FOR NURTURING LIVERPOOL'S ACTING AND WRITING TALENT. FOLLOWING A DIFFICULT PERIOD FOR BOTH THEATRES, THEY WERE MERGED INTO A SINGLE ORGANISATION IN 1999.

LIVERPOOL EVERYMAN AND PLAYHOUSE ARE CURRENTLY ENJOYING A CREATIVE REBIRTH. THE THEATRES HAVE RETURNED TO FULL-TIME PRODUCING, AND **MADE IN LIVERPOOL** IS ALREADY BEING RECOGNISED AS A STAMP OF THEATRICAL QUALITY ONCE AGAIN.

WITH THIS MAJOR EXPANSION IN PRODUCTION, A PASSIONATE COMMITMENT TO NEW WRITING, AND A RAPIDLY GROWING COMMUNITY PROGRAMME; WE ARE AT THE BEGINNING OF AN EXCITING JOURNEY TOWARDS LIVERPOOL'S YEAR AS EUROPEAN CAPITAL OF CULTURE IN 2008. OUR MISSION IS FOR THESE THEATRES TO BE FIRMLY ROOTED IN THEIR COMMUNITY, YET BOTH NATIONAL AND INTERNATIONAL IN SCOPE AND AMBITION.

EVERYMAN LIVERPOOL PLAYHOUSE

FOR FURTHER INFORMATION ON LIVERPOOL EVERYMAN AND PLAYHOUSE PLEASE CALL 0151 709 4776 OR SEE WWW.EVERYMANPLAYHOUSE.COM

EVERYMAN 13 HOPE STREET LIVERPOOL L1 9BH
PLAYHOUSE WILLIAMSON SQUARE LIVERPOOL L1 1EL

Comedy

**Best of 3...
Scouse stand-ups**

■ **Chris Cairns.** Razor-sharp wit hailing from the one and only Liverpool 8, and the city's 2003 Comedian of the Year.

■ **Keith Carter.** Man of many, many talents. Observe closely when he metamorphoses into cosmic uber-scally Nige, then try really hard not to laugh.

■ **Nathan McCullen.** Just 15 when he won Best New Comedian at the Liverpool Echo awards last year. How good's he gonna be when he grows up?

■ **The Laughterhouse BD**
13-15 Fenwick Street L2 7LS
Tel: (0151) 231 6881
Visit: laughterhouse.com
Established for three years now as a centre of comedic excellence, it's downstairs in the haunted (no kidding) cellar of the old alehouse. Four headline acts on a Saturday night and food (go for the red hot chilli platters) included in the price. Howard Marks has done a turn here. Mark Thomas topped the bill last August.

■ **The Pilgrim HQ**
34 Pilgrim Street L1 9HB
Tel: (0151) 709 2302
Beatle-tastic basement pub near to LIPA and the Anglican Cathedral. It's got a hugely popular Dead Good Poets Society and a new monthly comedy night upstairs that's starting to take off, run by drama students from John Moores University. Dig the Rubber Soul art.

■ **Rawhide @ Central Hall HQ**
Roscoe Gardens
Mount Pleasant L3 5SA
Tel: (0151) 726 2400
Visit: rawhidecomedy.com
Just moved from cool Blue on the Albert Dock to classical Grand Central (see page 91). The city's original stand-up show, in June it hosted the Liverpool leg of Channel 4's So You Think You're Funny? And the summer 2004 roll-call read like this: Reginald D Hunter, Brendan Dempsey, Junior Simpson, Mitch Benn, Ian Cognito, Steve Gribbin, Steve Best, Steve Hughes, Phil Nichol, Simon Evans, Marty Wilson, Colin Cole, Tony Burgess, Martin Beaumont and, of course, Keith Carter as Nige. We'd also like to draw your attention to Rawhide's Singing Hamsters. They sing the Rawhide theme, cost £7.50 and are 'supremely entertaining when drunk'. By all accounts.

Applause in the proceedings

Don't mean a thing if it ain't got that swing

187 Entertainment

Gigs

Best of 3... live music bars

■ **Blundell Street.** Just opposite Queen's Dock in a great converted warehouse for Rat Pack tribute acts par excellence through the weekend's early hours.

■ **Mustard Bar & Grill.** Smooth Sunday soul in what used to be called Holyoake Hall. The Beatles once played here way back in 1961.

■ **The Cavern.** Famous names and tribute bands aplenty. Ever seen the Fab Faux? Go on, you know you want to...

■ **Carling Academy CQ**
11-13 Hotham Street L3 5UF
Tel: (0151) 256 555
Visit: liverpool-academy.co.uk
You're just around the corner from Lime Street and the Empire Theatre (on the site of the old Lomax) in a rocking joint opened autumn 2003. The main auditorium holds 1,200 and hosts legends and upstarts in equal measure. The 500-capacity Academy 2 showcases rising talent, while Subculture is two rooms of rock and alternative music with guest deejays like the Von Bondies.

■ **Liverpool Academy HQ**
University of Liverpool
Guild of Students,
160 Mount Pleasant L69 7BR
Tel: (0151) 794 6868
Academy 1 is the biggie (2,000-capacity) that's been graced by Coldplay, Elvis Costello, Mercury Rev etc. Academy 2 holds 400 and has welcomed The Vines, The Fall, Lloyd Cole and Cooper Temple Clause. Last up, Academy 3 with space for 150 and a stage for upcoming acts. The entire venue also hosts Double Vision, a massive student night, every Monday. Oh for Tuesday lie-ins...

■ **Royal Court CQ**
1 Roe Street L1 1HL
Tel: (0151) 709 4321
Visit: royalcourttheatre.net
Fully restored to its former Art Deco glory and hosting drama once again (past performers include John Gielgud, Margot Fonteyn and Richard Burton) as well as pop. The basement lounge is a replica of the one on the original Queen Mary.

■ **Zanzibar RW**
43 Seel Street L1 4AZ
Tel: (0151) 707 0633
The Coral came out of this place. Noel Gallagher's hung out here when recording at Parr Street. Great for rising local talent and catching the next big thing.

The thrills

Liverpool loves its sport. Do you prefer to watch or join in?

■ There's the Grand National, no other horse race quite like it. Two football clubs with the kind of pedigree others pine for. And so many great golf courses it's ever-so-slightly embarrassing. An international tennis tournament, too, plus excellent sailing facilities (of course) and some first-class gyms and luxury spa centres. In the zone yet?

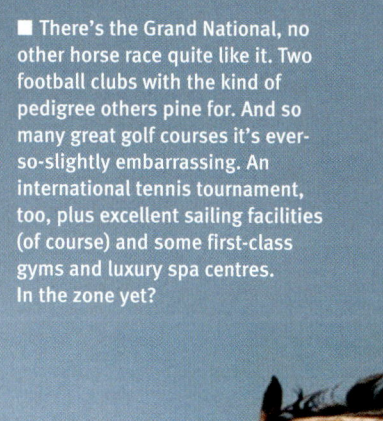

Sport

Horse racing

■ **Aintree Racecourse**
Ormskirk Road, Aintree L9 5AS
Tel: (0151) 523 2600
Visit: aintree.co.uk
The Grand National: four miles and 856 yards that have 600million viewers glued to their TV sets all over their globe. In 2004, Britons wagered a record £200million on a single day's sporting action for the first time as Amberleigh gave trainer Ginger McCain his first triumph since Red Rum's treble in the 70s. Aside from its blue riband race Aintree pulls in 30,000 punters on an average racing day – well ahead of Ascot and Cheltenham – and £30million has been set aside for two huge grandstands and a new ring parade by 2007.

■ **Haydock Park**
Newton-le-Willows WA12 0HQ
Tel: 01942 72596
Visit: haydock-park.com
Over 250 years old and one of the country's premier racecourses. Every year there are 31 meetings featuring both Flat and National Hunt races and attracting 250,000 people. Off Junction 23 of the M6.

Football

■ **Everton FC**
Goodison Park L4 4EL
Tickets: 0870 442 1878
Visit: evertonfc.com
If you know your history, this is the first football club in England to spend 100 years in the top flight – a feat celebrated in 2003 – and the one that's given the world two magnificent centre-forwards from different eras with the same world-class credentials. Dixie Dean was the first and only player to score 60 league goals in a season, back in 1928. Powerpack teenager and England Euro 2004 sensation Wayne Rooney surely has a host of records in front of him. After the glory years of the mid-80s, the Blues have had their barren spells of late. But their pedigree is second-to-none and their followers remain as passionate and loyal as ever. Get down to Goodison.

■ **Liverpool FC**
Anfield Road L4 0TH
Ticket hotline: 0870 220 2345
Visit: liverpoolfc.tv

There are the lucky, lucky ones who got to stand on the Spion Kop and sing Queen's We Are The Champions when it really was no1 in the charts and Liverpool had just clinched another title on some unremembered late spring evening. And there are the ones who have supported the team all their lives and not yet seen them play.

Either way, the feeling is the same when they've veered right from Scotland Road, up Everton Valley and onto Walton Breck Road, and got that first glimpse of the Kop Grandstand, its massive bulk dwarfing the adjacent terraced housing. Welcome to one of the most legendary sporting venues on the planet, the home of Liverpool Football Club and a shrine for hundreds of thousands of pilgrims worldwide. Arsenal, Chelsea and Manchester United may joust for the Premiership's top spot, but this club always stands alone.

Outside the superstore is a statue of Bill Shankly, mythical manager in the Swinging Sixties. Both 'the Shanks' and successor Bob Paisley — the only coach to guide a team to three European Cup victories — are commemorated by giant gates either side of the stadium, which also has a Hillsborough Memorial.

The club's success on the pitch is phenomenal and unsurpassed. Most recently six trophies were won under previous manager Gerard Houllier, and the all-time haul of silverware is: four European Cups, three UEFA Cups, two European Super Cups, a record 18 League Championships, six FA Cups and seven League Cups. Many of the medals and plenty of memorabilia — from superstars like Michael Owen and Steven Gerrard — are on show at the museum, where you'll also experience the electric atmosphere of the old Kop and the learn about the Liverpool anthem You'll Never Walk Alone.

A new 60,000-seater stadium is planned for the near future, so get up to the original Anfield while you still can.

191 Sport

England's Golf Coast...

■ Merseyside has over 40 quality golf courses, including some of the UK's most challenging and beautiful venues, nestling between the pace of urban life and ruggedness of the coastline. Seven of them are leading Championship venues. As well Royal Liverpool and Royal Birkdale, there's Hillside in Southport and Formby Hall, host to the 2004 Curtis Cup. Now a new Festival of Golf is being staged at courses in Sefton and Wirral every year until at least 2006. Central to the week-long event will be the Merseyside English Seniors Open, forming part of the European Seniors Tour with household names like Sam Torrance, Tony Jacklin and Bernhard Gallacher. There's more at englandsgolfcoast.com.

Golf

■ **Royal Birkdale**
Waterloo Road, Southport PR8 2LX
Tel: 01704 567920
Visit: royalbirkdale.com
Considered to be the best course in the country, Birkdale and its mighty sand dunes will stage the Open Championship for the ninth time in 2008. In the past it's seen greats like Arnold Palmer, Lee Trevino, Tom Watson and Mark O'Meara all lift the famous claret jug.

■ **Royal Liverpool**
Meols Drive, Hoylake CH47 4AL
Tel: (0151) 632 3101
Visit: royal-liverpool-golf.com
Another outstanding seaside links with a distinguished history (only Westward Ho! in Devon is older). It looks benign, plays tough and is likely to attract 250,000 people and 500million TV viewers for the British Open in 2006. It was on this quite corner of the Wirral in 1930 that Bobby Jones won the second leg of his famous Grand Slam.

Tennis

■ **Calderstones Park**
Childwall L18 3JD
Tel: (0151) 227 5940
Visit: liverpooltennis.co.uk
A gloriously green setting with 36 grass courts and a 5,000-seater stadium with a lakeside backdrop. In mid-June it hosts the Liverpool International Tennis Tournament, an eight-man, round-robin warm-up for Wimbledon with star names aplenty, and a Legends event that's featured Ilie Nastase, among others.

Cricket

■ **Liverpool Cricket Club**
Aigburth Road,
Grassendale L19 3QF
Tel: (0151) 427 2930
Visit: liverpoolcricketclub.co.uk
Stages Lancashire CC fixtures and was a firm favourite with Don Bradman. The pavilion has function rooms with views to the Welsh hills. As the playful website says, 'There is no finer way to spend a Saturday afternoon than watching a cricket match from the balcony with a pint of our finest beer at hand'...

Sailing and watersports

■ **Liverpool Yacht Club**
Coburg Wharf L3 4BP
Tel: (0151) 281 8186
Visit: lyc.org.uk
Located in the Marina & Harbourside Club (340 permanent pontoon berths), half-a-nautical-mile from the scuba-diving centre at Albert Dock, with races every other weekend on the Mersey and out to the Irish Sea. There are also courses for newcomers and regular day-trips and weekend cruises along the beautiful coasts of North and West Wales, the Isle of Man, Cumbria and Scotland. And you can hire the clubhouse for anything from a buffet to five-course meal.

Aviation

■ **Helicentre Liverpool**
John Lennon Airport L24 5GA
Tel: (0151) 448 0388
Visit: helicentre.com
Take a tour of Liverpool in a helicopter, or a flying lesson as a thrilling one-off experience or first step to a Private Pilots Licence.

Climbing

■ **Awesome Walls Centre**
Athol Street L5 9XT
Tel: (0151) 298 2422
Visit: awesomewalls.co.uk
A mile from the city-centre, one of the largest indoor climbing centres in Europe with walls and routes to suit all skill levels.

Fitness and well being

■ **Absolution Gym**
Britannia Pavilion,
Albert Dock L3 4AD
Tel: (0151) 707 9333
Gym, sauna, steam room, professional beauty treatments and spa with special one-day guest packages.

■ **Ark Health & Fitness**
Radisson SAS Hotel,
107 Old Hall Street L3 9BD
Tel: (0151) 966 1500
Visit: radissonsas.com
Three-levels with pool, jacuzzi, steam room, sauna, gym and beauty treatments in one of the city's newest and most prestigious hotels.

■ **Club Spa**
Crowne Plaza Hotel,
St Nicholas Place L3 1QW
Tel: (0151) 243 8243
Visit: cpliverpool.com
Therapeutic massage that enhances well-being and reduces tension, plus aromatherapy massage to treat a range of physiological conditions.

■ **David Lloyd**
6 The Aerodrome, Speke L24 8QD
Tel: (0151) 494 4000
Visit: davidlloydleisure.co.uk
Arguably the most comprehensive health, fitness and racquets facility in Liverpool, located in a remarkable building – a renovation of one of the hangars on the old airport site.

■ **Greens Health & Fitness**
1 Riverside Drive L3 4EN
Tel: (0151) 707 6000
Visit: greensonline.co.uk
Unisex beauty treatments, pool, aroma steamroom, sun showers and exercise rooms with women-only classes, plus bar, brasserie and take-home food service.

■ **Leisure Club**
Marriott City Centre Hotel,
Queen Square L1 1RH
Tel: (0151) 476 8000
Swimming pool, solarium, fitness centre plus aromatherapy, reflexology and massage.

Holistic

■ **Alternative therapies**
Astanga Vinyasa Yoga
13 Arrad Street L7 7BQ
Tel: (0151) 639 5776
Classical postures in a continuous sequence. But bring your own mat!

■ **The Health Place**
Blackburne House,
Hope Street L8 7PE
Tel: (0151) 709 4356
Visit: blackburnehouse.co.uk
Holistic health and fitness for women, with a range of therapies.

■ **Massage & Flotation Centre**
66A Lord Street L2 1TD
Tel: (0151) 709 9701
Visit: themassagecentre.co.uk
Specialising in flotation therapy, plus massage treatments, body wraps and special pamper days.

■ **Chinese Acupuncture Centre**
31 Rodney Street L1 9EH
Tel: (0151) 703 2938
Newly-opened, initial consultations and 45-minute sessions.

Out of town

You are now 50 miles, as the Liver Bird flies, from the highest peak in Wales (Snowdon) and 65 miles from England's biggest mountain (Scafell Pike in the Lake District). In-between, there's rather a lot going on...

Greater Liverpool and Lancashire

■ South along Riverside Drive from the city-centre is the serene promenade at Otterspool, and later Halewood Triangle Country Park (among the oldest surviving native woodland in Merseyside), plus the idyllic splendour of Speke Hall and iconic refurbishment of Speke Matchworks.

To the north-east there's Croxteth Hall & Country Park, an historic mansion in a 500-acre wooded park, and Knowsley, home to the National Wildflower Centre and the Safari Park, the first of its kind to open close to a large city and a haven for lions, tigers, elephants and rhino – all viewed from the comfort of your vehicle.

Due north from Waterloo is the Sefton Coast with its string of nature reserves. Formby Point is the fourth largest dune system in the country and home to one of Britain's last colonies of red squirrels and natterjack toads, as well as a wonderful array of birdlife such as oystercatchers, sanderlings, yellowhammers and greater spotted woodpeckers.

On to the elegant seaside resort of Southport, approximately 20 miles from Liverpool, with golden sands, green lawns, Victorian shopping arcades and a climate that boasts more sunshine hours than anywhere else in the North West of England.

Wirral and Cheshire

■ Directly opposite the Pier Head is Birkenhead, with its Norman Priory dating from 1150 and Historic Warships Centre at East Float Dock – check out the big, brooding U-Boat 534, the only German submarine raised from the seabed after being sunk by the Allies.

Nearby is the riverside development Twelve Quays from where two of Liverpool's three freight and passenger services to Ireland operate, and further north Seacombe's Aquarium (octopus, lobsters, crabs and a giant conger eel) and new £8million Astronomy & Space Centre, then New Brighton promenade and Fort Perch Rock.

Head south for Port Sunlight Heritage Centre (over 900 listed buildings and landscaped gardens) and Ellesmere Port's Boat Museum and Blue Planet Aquarium, featuring an underwater tunnel and huge window onto one the largest collections of sharks in the whole of Europe.

The other side of Wirral boasts West Kirby Marine Lake and promenade, and seal-spotting on the nearby Hilbre Islands Local Nature Reserve.

Due south is Wirral Country Park in Thurstaston (and its superb views across the Dee Estuary to Wales), the picturesque resort of Parkgate and Ness Botanic Gardens in Neston (owned by the University of Liverpool). From here you can see Moel Famau, the first big peak in North Wales, in its country park of gentle slopes and teeming wildlife. And you're a matter of minutes from the walled city of Chester, easily accessed on special trips by Merseyrail.

197 **Out of town**

PREMIER EVENTS & FESTIVALS 2004
there's something for everyone...

North West Historic Car Rally	24-25 July
Merseyside International Street Festival	24-25 July
Summer Classics – 'Music in the Park'	30-31 July
B.R.A Search For A Star – Heats	5 Aug - 2 Sept
Woodvale International Rally	7-8 August
Southport Flower Show	19-22 August
Southport Air Show & Military Display	11-12 September
B.R.A Search For A Star – NW Regional Final	18 September
24 Hour Yacht Race	18-19 September
English Seniors Open	24-26 September
Pleasureland British Musical Fireworks Championships	8-9 October
Southport Comedy Festival	14-17 & 21-23 Oct
Halloween Party, Pleasureland	31 October
Bonfire Party, Pleasureland	5 November
Meols Hall Bonfire & Grand Firework Display	6 November
B.R.A Search For A Star – National Final	20 November
Christmas Lights Switch-on & Grand Parade	7 November

Note all dates are provisional and may be subject to change.

For more information about festivals and events in Southport, call our Events Hotline:
01704 395511 Please quote: LTG04

For an accommodation guide call:
01704 533333 (24hrs) Please quote: LTG04

or visit our website:
www.VisitSouthport.com

Southport Premier Events and Festivals

Sefton Council
This project is part funded by the European Union under the Objective One Programme for Merseyside

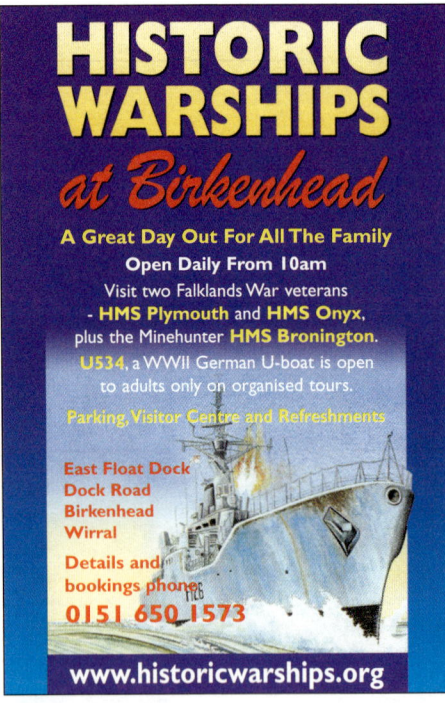

HISTORIC WARSHIPS
at Birkenhead

A Great Day Out For All The Family
Open Daily From 10am

Visit two Falklands War veterans
- **HMS Plymouth** and **HMS Onyx**,
plus the Minehunter **HMS Bronington**.
U534, a WWII German U-boat is open to adults only on organised tours.

Parking, Visitor Centre and Refreshments

East Float Dock
Dock Road
Birkenhead
Wirral

Details and bookings phone
0151 650 1573

www.historicwarships.org

Super accommodation at budget prices...

Holme Leigh
Guest House

Single rooms from £17 per night
Twin rooms from £34 per night
(continental breakfast included)

0151 734 2216
www.HolmeLeigh.com

In association with:

NHS Walk in Centres

Details

Liverpool. The nitty gritty. If it's out there, it's in here. Your handy directory of practical information...

199 Details

Need more help? Look for Liverpool's information society...

■ You'll find a system of information panels all over the city-centre designed to make discovery easier. There are 81 fingerposts and 37 interpretation panels featuring a mapping system displaying icon buildings in 3D and areas within six minutes walk – all in clear colours for visually-impaired people with clear identification of steps and areas inaccessible to wheelchair users.

On Church Street (Shopping Centre) you'll discover more help at one of six pavement pods that open up a whole new e-world for visitors and residents alike. Use it to find out about tourism, culture, sport, council services and jobs, or to contact friends and relatives in the UK or overseas via free email, text messages and photomail (remember the telephone area code for Liverpool is 0151; if you're calling overseas the prefix is +44). Information is available in English, Spanish, French, Chinese and Somali, and the other pods are on Upper Parliament Street (Liverpool 8), West Derby Road (Tuebrook), Breck Road (Anfield), Allerton Road (Allerton) and Moss Way (Croxteth).

Outside FACT (Rope Walks) are five flashing beacons called metroscopes – the first UK sculptures to feed off information from the web, beaming live news from Liverpool's sister cities Shanghai, Cologne, Odessa and Dublin. And The 08 Place is a new focal point for the Capital of Culture experience situated on Whitechapel, close to the Met Quarter Development. It provides tourist advice and information, merchandise and a tickets/booking service.

Tourist information
■ General enquiries
Tel: (0151) 709 5111/8111
or: 0906 680 6886
(calls cost 25p per minute)
■ Queen Square Centre
Mon-Sat 9am-5.30pm;
Sun & Bank Holidays
10.30am-4.30pm
■ Albert Dock Centre
Atlantic Pavillion,
Albert Dock L3
Daily 10am-5.30pm
■ Liverpool John Lennon Airport
Oct-Mar: daily 5am-11pm
Apr-Sept: daily 4am-12am

Accommodation service
■ Free accommodation booking
Tel: (0151) 709 8111
or: 0845 601 1125 (local call rate)
Visit: visitliverpool.com

Left luggage
■ Lime Street Station L1
Tel: (0151) 702 2219
Daily 7am-9pm (£4.50 per item)

Banks and exchange
■ Most of the city-centre's large hotels have bureau de change facilities for visitors. You can also change money at Liverpool's larger post offices. Basic opening hours Mon-Fri 9.30am-4.30pm.
■ Barclays
Whitechapel L1
Mon-Sat 9am-5pm.
■ American Express
54 Lord Street L2
(0151) 702 4501
Mon-Fri 9am-5.30pm; Sat 9am-5pm
■ Thomas Cook
HSBC, 4 Dale Street L2
Commission free

Post offices
■ Mon-Sat 9am-5.30pm
(unless stated)
■ Corn Exchange
India Building, Water Street L2
Mon-Fri 9am-5.30pm
■ Exchange
82 Old Hall Street L3
Mon-Fri 8am-5.30pm

■ Leece Street
35/37 Leece Street L1
Mon-Fri 8.45am-5.30pm;
Sat 8.45am-12.30pm
■ Liverpool St Johns
St John's Centre, Houghton Way L1
Foreign currency exchange available
■ Lyceum
1 Bold Street L1

Internet Cafés
■ Café Latte.net
4 South Hunter Street L1
Tel: (0151) 708 9610
Mon-Fri 8am-9pm;
Sat-Sun 9am-5.30pm
■ Planet Electra Internet Café
36 London Road L3
Tel: (0151) 280 7000
Mon-Fri 8am-9pm;
Sat-Sun 9am-5.30pm

Shop opening times
Mon-Sat 9am-5.30pm;
Sun 11am-4.30pm
Small, independent shops
and markets may differ.

Details 200

What's to do...

■ Central Liverpool Primary Care Trust is an NHS organisation that guides the work of doctor's surgeries and other local health services and makes sure that hospital care and other specialist treatment is available to people when they need it. Our Walk-In Centres are on Great Charlotte Row in the city-centre and Crystal Close off St Oswalds Street in Old Swan. These are local facilities where no appointment is necessary, offering quick access to a range of NHS services, including advice, information and treatment for a range of minor injuries and illnesses (these could include cuts and bruises, strains and sprains, minor infections, skin complaints). Patients do not need to be registered with a GP to receive treatment, and we're open from 7am to 10pm, Monday to Friday, and 9am to 10pm, Saturday and Sunday.

Advertorial

DOLBY HOTEL

FROM £38.00 PER ROOM

- Situated on the famous Liverpool waterfront.
- Five minutes walk from the busy Albert Dock and only ten minutes from the city centre.
- 65 modern equipped bedrooms, all en suite (sleeping upto three)
- Half the rooms boasting panoramic views of the river
- Dock side Lounge Bar serving food and drink
- Guest Lounge
- Free parking on site

Dolby Hotel, Queens Dock, Liverpool L3 4DE. Tel. 0151 708 7272
www.dolbyhotels.co.uk
Email: liverpool@dolbyhotels.co.uk

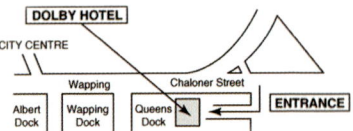

ECHO

Something for everyone six days a week

DISCOVER **SOMETHING NEW** Six days a week

LIVERPOOL DAILY POST

Getting here

■ Liverpool's location makes it easily accessible from all parts of the UK. There's a daily airlink between London and John Lennon Airport, which offers an increasing number of scheduled international destinations (Alicante, Amsterdam, Basel, Barcelona, Belfast, Berlin, Cologne, Dublin, Geneva, Gerona, Isle of Man, Madrid, Malaga, Nice, Palma, Paris) and is well-connected to the city-centre. Regular ferry services run from Liverpool to Ireland, while Lime Street train station is a major rail terminus on the West Coast Line from London Euston and is also linked to Manchester Airport via the Merseyrail City Line. For cars and coaches, the motorway network is linked via the M62, M58, M57 and M3/M56.

■ **John Lennon Airport**
Tel: **(0151) 288 4000**
or: **0870 750 8484**
Visit: **liverpooljohnlennonairport.com**
In Speke, six miles to the south-east of the city-centre.

■ **VLM London-Liverpool**
Tel: **(0151) 236 9696**
or: **020 7476 6677**
Visit: **flyvlm.com**
Five flights every weekday between JLA and London City Airport in Docklands (three miles from Canary). A fast 15-min check-in and fares starting from £36.90 one-way.

■ **AirportXpress 500**
Tel: **(0151) 236 7676**
Buses from airport to city centre. From 5.15am-12.15am, 15 minutes past and

15 minutes to every hour (£2 adult, £1 child) seven days a week.
■ **National Rail Enquiries**
Tel: **0845 748 4950**
Visit: **thetrainline.co.uk**
■ **National Express Coaches**
Norton Street L3
Tel: **0870 580 8080**
Visit: **nationalexpress.com**
Operating regular services from all major towns and cities in the UK.
■ **Norse Merchant Ferries**
Tel: **(0151) 944 1010**
Regular service from Belfast and Dublin.
■ **P&O Irish Sea**
Tel: **0870 242 4777**
Visit: **poirishsea.com**
Early morning and overnight crossings from Dublin to Liverpool Freeport (Bootle) on the Norbank and Norbay ferries with two restaurant areas and lounges, a bar and en suite cabins.
■ **SeaCat/Isle of Man Steam Packet Co**

Tel: **0870 552 3523**
Visit: **steam-packet.com**
Room for 774 passengers and 175 cars onboard the smooth 'n' sleek SuperSeaCat from Dublin and the Isle of Man to Liverpool's Princes Dock Landing Stage (Pier Head). The engines, incidentally, were built by GEC Alstrom of Merseyside. Mar-Nov: daily service to Douglas IOM (2hrs 50mins) and Dublin (4hrs). Nov-Mar: weekend ferry to Douglas (4hrs).

Getting around

The River Mersey can be crossed by ferry, the two car tunnels and Merseyrail underground network, with regular trains between James Street and Hamilton Square. There's a comprehensive bus and train system, and a new tram scheme featuring a 10-stop city-centre loop will be fully operational by 2007.
■ **Traveline Merseyside**
Tel: **(0151) 236 7676**
(information on all local bus and train services)
or: **0870 608 2608** (public transport services throughout England, Scotland and Wales)
■ **Merseytravel**
Tel: **(0151) 236 7676**
Visit: **merseytravel.gov.uk**
Information, updates and tickets for public transport on buses, trains and ferries. Fares vary depending on journey and company used. Pay at point of departure or purchase Saveaway tickets from train stations, Merseytravel centres at Queen Square, Paradise Street and 24 Hatton Garden or from newsagents and post offices. Saveaway Tickets one-day passes for use on buses, trains and ferries from 9.30am-4pm and after 6pm, all day weekends and Bank Holidays. £2.10-£2.70 adult, £1.60-£1.90 under 15s.
■ **Merseyrail**
Tel: **(0151) 236 7676**
or: **0870 608 2608**
(calls charged at national rate)
Visit: **merseyrail.org**
Extensive urban rail network connecting the city of Liverpool with the rest of Merseyside: Southport, Ormskirk, Kirkby and Hunts Cross on the Northern Line; New Brighton, West Kirby, Chester and Ellesmere Port on the Wirral Line, including four city-centre underground stations (James Street, Moorfields, Lime Street and Central) and connections to other towns and cities.

203 Details

Buses
Most major attractions can be reached by the city's SMART bus service, single-decker buses with facilities for wheelchairs and pushchairs. Main bus depots at Paradise Street and Queen Square.
■ Mersey Ferries
Tel: (0151) 236 7676
Visit: merseyferries.co.uk
Daily commuter service from Pier Head to Seacombe and Woodside on the Wirral. Mon-Fri 7.45-9.15am & 4.15-7.15pm, with hourly River Explorer Cruise service 10am-3pm; Sat-Sun 9.05-9.35am & 7pm, River Explorer Cruise 10am-6pm.

Taxis
■ The main black cab ranks are at Lime Street Station, James Street Station, Adelphi Hotel, Whitechapel, Sir Thomas Street, Great George Street and Chinatown.

Private hire taxis
■ Davy Liver Ltd
Tel: (0151) 709 2031/4646
■ Dial-A-Cab
Tel: (0151) 480 8000
■ Mersey Cabs
Tel: (0151) 298 2222

Car Hire
■ National Car Rental
Tel: (0151) 259 1316
nationalcar.com
■ Skydrive UK Ltd
Tel: (0151) 448 0000
or: 07801 423500

■ Absolute Class Chauffeur Services
Tel: 0800 587 4575
Visit: absoluteclass.uk.com
■ Ansome Heritage Hire
(0151) 531 6947
■ Elite Chauffeur Services
Tel: (0151) 292 8435
Visitl: elitechauffeurs.co.uk
■ First Company
Tel: (0151) 236 5640
Visit: 1stcompany.com
■ INTX
Tel: (0151) 727 7000
Tel: intxuk.com

Coach Hire
■ Matthews Travel
Tel: (0151) 342 1833
Visit: coach2hire.com
■ Maghull Coaches
Tel: (0151) 933 2324
Visit: maghullcoaches.co.uk
■ Maypole Coaches
Tel: (0151) 547 2713

Car Parks
■ British Car Parks
Oldham Street L1
Tel: (0151) 709 8727
24-hour multi-storey
■ Pall Mall L3
Tel: (0151) 236 5738
Mon-Fri 7.30am-7.30pm
■ Newquay L1
Tel: (0151) 227 1274
Multi-storey Mon-Sat 7am-7pm
■ Lime Street L1
Tel: (0151) 709 7014
24-hour multi-storey
■ Paradise Street L1
Tel: (0151) 707 2455
24-hour multi-storey
■ John Lennon Airport L24
Tel: (0151) 486 5689
24-hour multi-storey

Travellers with disabilities
■ Merseylink
Tel: (0151) 709 1929
Transport information service for people with disabilities.

■ Shopmobility
Tel: (0151) 708 9993
■ Dial UK
Tel: 01302 310 123
Information and advice line

Emergency services
■ For police, fire service, ambulance or coastguard in an emergency, call 999 or 112. For a free home fire safety check, call 0800 731 5958.
■ Merseyside Police HQ
Canning Place
Tel: (0151) 709 6010
Visit: merseyside.police.uk
■ Merseyside Fire Service HQ
Bridle Road, Bootle
Tel: (0151) 296 4000
Visit: merseyfire.gov.uk
■ Transco Gas Emergency Service
Tel: 0800 111 999
■ United Utilities (Water Leakline)
Tel: 0800 330 033

Hospitals and medical
■ NHS Direct
Tel: 0845 4747
Visit: nhsdirect.nhs.uk
Round-the-clock service providing immediate and confidential health advice and information, plus dental advice.

Hospitals – Accident & Emergency
With 24-hour casualty departments:
■ Royal Liverpool
Prescot Street L3
Tel: (0151) 706 2000

What's to do…

■ Wherever you are in Liverpool, an Arriva bus won't be too far away. Over the past three years Arriva North West and Wales has invested over £20million in its fleet, making it among the most modern in the UK. This means that nearly half of our services in Merseyside are operated by easy-access, low-floor vehicles. Last November we launched 'Le bus', a unique concept with routes that offer customers high-frequency services with improved visual display, CCTV and a dedicated team of specially trained drivers – many of whom are learning new languages to help welcome visitors to the city. In the meantime, the success of Arriva's latest prize draw, which celebrates Liverpool's 2008 Capital of Culture victory, has left many customers checking their bus tickets each time they board. To enter, customers must first check the serial number. If that number is 2008, they send it to our head office to be entered in to the draw for a prize of – you've guessed it – £2,008!

205 **Advertorial**

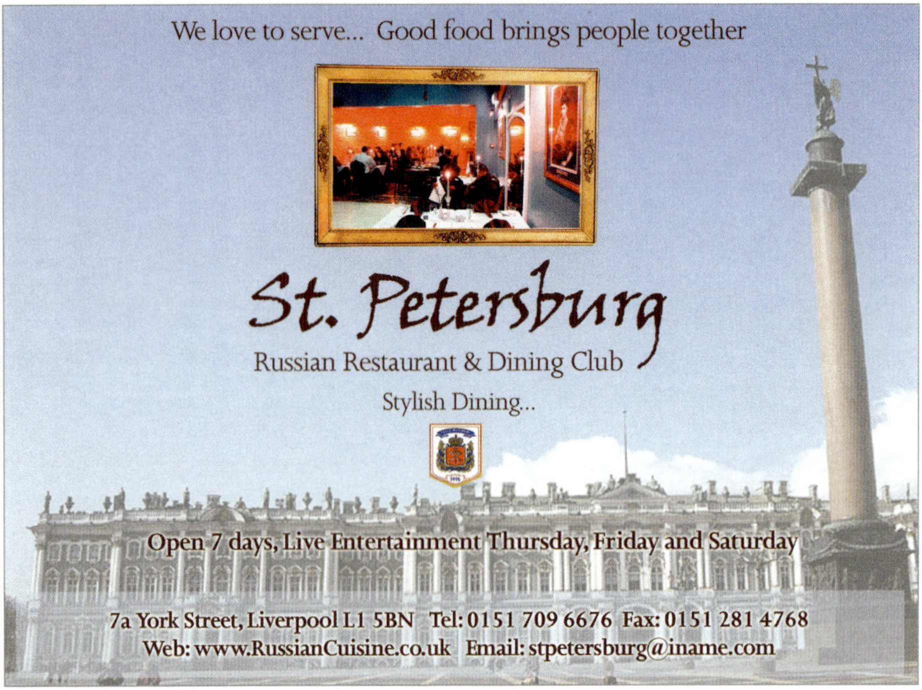

We love to serve... Good food brings people together
St. Petersburg
Russian Restaurant & Dining Club
Stylish Dining...
Open 7 days, Live Entertainment Thursday, Friday and Saturday
7a York Street, Liverpool L1 5BN Tel: 0151 709 6676 Fax: 0151 281 4768
Web: www.RussianCuisine.co.uk Email: stpetersburg@iname.com

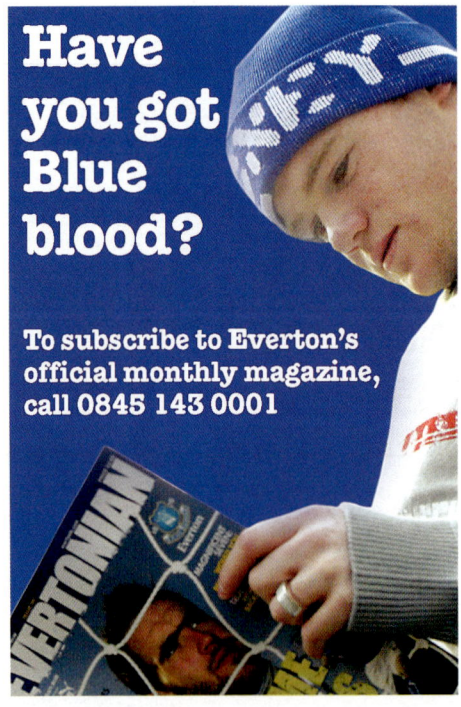

Have you got Blue blood?
To subscribe to Everton's official monthly magazine, call 0845 143 0001
EVERTONIAN

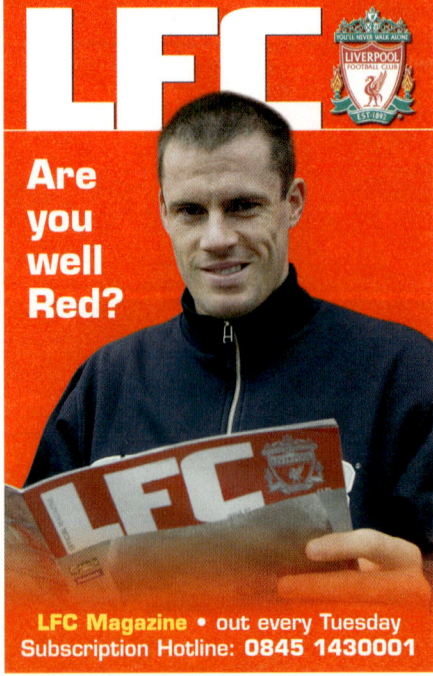

LFC
Are you well Red?
LFC Magazine • out every Tuesday
Subscription Hotline: 0845 1430001

- University Hospital Aintree
Lower Lane L9
Tel: (0151) 525 5980
- Alder Hey Hospital (children only)
Eaton Road L12
Tel: (0151) 228 4811

Walk-In Centres
- General enquiries
Tel: (0151) 285 3535
Primary Care Trusts, or PCTs, offer treatment and consultations for minor injuries and illnesses with NHS doctors and nurses. Health advice and information is also available on other local services, including out-of-hours doctors, dentists and chemists. No appointment necessary. Mon-Fri 7am-10pm; Sat-Sun 9am-10pm.
- Liverpool City
Unit 4, Great Charlotte Street L1
- Old Swan
Crystal Close, St Oswald Street L13

Specialist hospitals
- Women's Hospital
Crown Street L8
Tel: (0151) 708 9988
Teaching hospital caring for mothers and babies.
- Dental Hospital
Pembroke Place L3
Tel: (0151) 706 5050
Mon-Fri 8am-5.30pm

Late-night Chemists
- Moss Chemists
68/70 London Road L3
Tel: (0151) 709 5271
Daily 8am-11pm

- Moss Pharmacy
19 Prescot Road L7
Tel: (0151) 263 2486
Mon-Fri 9.30am-9pm;
Sat 9.30am-8pm

Helplines
- Alcoholics Anonymous
Tel: 0845 769 7555
- Brook Advisory Centre
Tel: (0151) 207 4000
Free confidential advice on birth control for young people.
- Calm
Tel: 0800 585858
Free and confidential help and advice for young men.
- Childline
Tel: 0800 1111
- Merseyside Drugs Council
Tel: (0151) 709 0074
Visit: drugscouncil.com
- National Drugs Helpline
Tel: 0800 776 600
- Gamblers Anonymous
Tel: 0161 976 5000
- Gay Youth R Out
Tel: (0151) 709 6660
Information and support for young people.
- Mersey AIDS Line
Tel: (0151) 709 9000
- Office of the Immigration Services Commissioner
Tel: 0845 000 0046
Visit: oisc.gov.uk
Information and advice on regulatory requirements.
- Pregnancy Advisory Service
Tel: 0161 228 1887
- Samaritans
Tel: (0151) 708 8888
- Young Person's Advisory Service
Tel: (0151) 707 1025

Childcare
- Dukes & Duchesses
Dukes Terrace, Duke Street L1
Tel: (0151) 709 1186
Purpose-built, city-centre day nursery with full and part-time places.

Liverpool city council
- Municipal Buildings
Dale Street L1
Tel: (0151) 233 3000 (general)
Tel: (0151) 233 3001 (environmental)
Tel: (0151) 233 3004 (registrar)
Tel: (0151) 233 3010 (social services)
Visit: liverpool.gov.uk
Mon-Fri 8am-10pm;
Sat-Sun 10am-6pm

Consulates
- Consulate of the Cape Verde Republic
20 Stanley Street L1
Tel: (0151) 236 0206
- Cónsul Honorario de Chile
4 Hardman Street L1
Tel: (0151) 708 6036
- Consulate of the Dominican Republic
539 Martins Building, Water Street L2
Tel: (0151) 236 0722
- Honorary Consulate of Finland
100 Wavertree Boulevard L7
Tel: (0151) 228 8161
- Consulate of Hungary
43 Rodney Street L1
Tel: (0151) 708 9088
- Vice Consul of Iceland
Norwich House, Water Street L1
- Honorary Consulate of Italy
4 Mortimer Street, Birkenhead
Tel: (0151) 666 2886
- Honorary Consulate of the Netherlands
Cotton Exchange, Old Hall Street L3
Tel: (0151) 227 5161

207 Details

Word up

Some recommended reading...

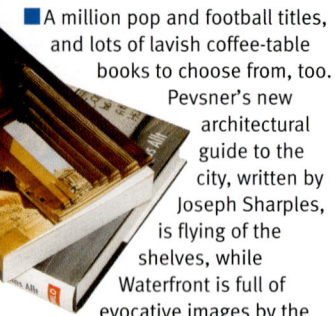

■ A million pop and football titles, and lots of lavish coffee-table books to choose from, too. Pevsner's new architectural guide to the city, written by Joseph Sharples, is flying of the shelves, while Waterfront is full of evocative images by the award-winning photographer Guy Woodland, who also took the pics for Liverpool: The First 1,000 Years, by Arabella McIntyre-Brown – first published in 2001 and the complete history of the city. Check out, too, Liverpool: City of Architecture, by Professor Quentin Hughes, and the recently updated Liverpool: A People's History, by Peter Aughton.

Musos need look no further than Liverpool Wondrous Place: Music from the Cavern to the Coral, by Paul Du Noyer, the ultimate encyclopaedia of the Scouse sound now out in paperback with a foreword by Sir Paul McCartney. For popular fiction, try Outlaws, by Kevin Sampson, a tense thriller set in South Liverpool and told in the city's vernacular. Brass, by Helen Walsh, is another bare-knuckle urban adventure, while The Boys from the Mersey, by Nicholas Allt, charts the Continental escapades of Liverpool FC's streetwise supporters in the late 70s.

The city has all the major booksellers and some fascinating second-hand stores around the top of Bold Street (Rope Walks), but arguably the best source for local writing is in the Bluecoat Arts Centre on School Lane (Shopping Centre). It also has its own publishing house, Bluecoat Press. In Central Library, too, you'll find some real gems among its superb selection on the second floor. Scully, by the legendary Alan Bleasdale, is a seminal Liverpool classic first published in 1975 and chronicling the adventures of a teenage scallywag.

Look for anthologies by Adrian Henri, Roger McGough and Brian Patten, the poets of the Mersey Sound (the pop movement of the 1960s). And for great bedside reading try the prolific Richard Whittington-Egan, a former Daily Post columnist, and Frank Kane, the king of Liverpool murder and mystery.

Among the classics, you'll find passages about Liverpool in Daniel Defoe's A Tour Through England and Wales, as well as Billy Budd and Redburn by Herman Melville (author of Moby Dick), and more recently Nicholas Monsarrat's The Cruel Sea.

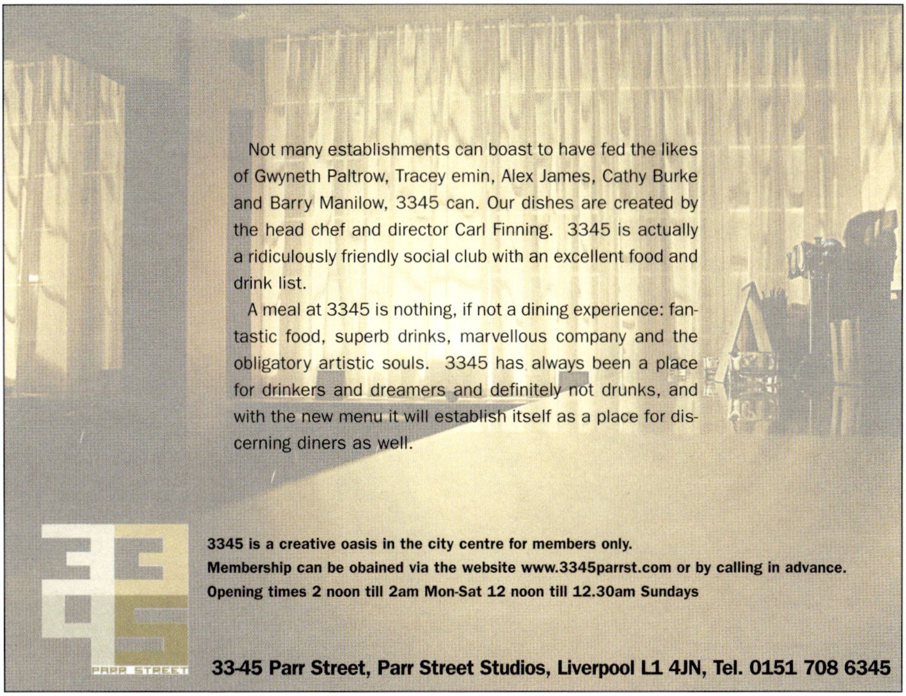

Not many establishments can boast to have fed the likes of Gwyneth Paltrow, Tracey emin, Alex James, Cathy Burke and Barry Manilow, 3345 can. Our dishes are created by the head chef and director Carl Finning. 3345 is actually a ridiculously friendly social club with an excellent food and drink list.

A meal at 3345 is nothing, if not a dining experience: fantastic food, superb drinks, marvellous company and the obligatory artistic souls. 3345 has always been a place for drinkers and dreamers and definitely not drunks, and with the new menu it will establish itself as a place for discerning diners as well.

3345 is a creative oasis in the city centre for members only. Membership can be obained via the website www.3345parrst.com or by calling in advance. Opening times 2 noon till 2am Mon-Sat 12 noon till 12.30am Sundays

33-45 Parr Street, Parr Street Studios, Liverpool L1 4JN, Tel. 0151 708 6345

www.pacificbarandgrill.com

Pacific Bar & Grill, Temple St, (off Victoria St) City Centre, Liverpool, L2 5RH.
Tel: 0151 236 0270   Fax: 0151 236 8287

"Puschka is **extremely popular** with Liverpool residents for its **delicious food** combined with **excellent,** unpretentious **service.** Although it is **smart,** anyone who eats there feels they can **relax.**"

The **Independent**
'Best of Liverpool 2004'

PUSCHKA
16 Rodney Street
Liverpool L1 2TE
www.puschka.co.uk
+44 (0)151 708 8698

supporting Smoke-free Liverpool

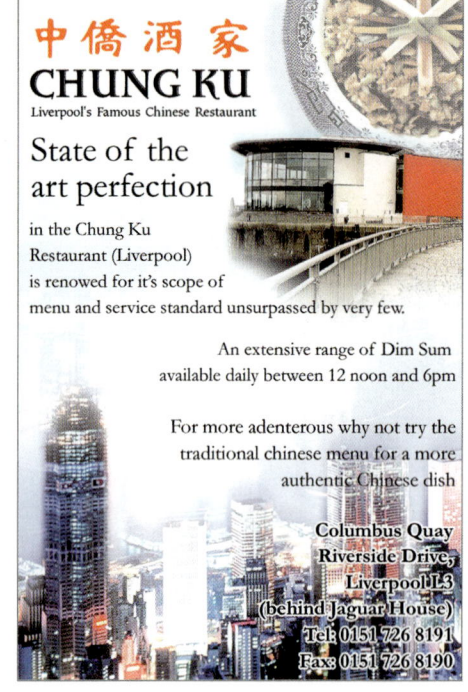

中僑酒家
CHUNG KU
Liverpool's Famous Chinese Restaurant

State of the art perfection

in the Chung Ku Restaurant (Liverpool) is renowned for it's scope of menu and service standard unsurpassed by very few.

An extensive range of Dim Sum available daily between 12 noon and 6pm

For more adenterous why not try the traditional chinese menu for a more authentic Chinese dish

Columbus Quay
Riverside Drive,
Liverpool L3
(behind Jaguar House)
Tel: 0151 726 8191
Fax: 0151 726 8190

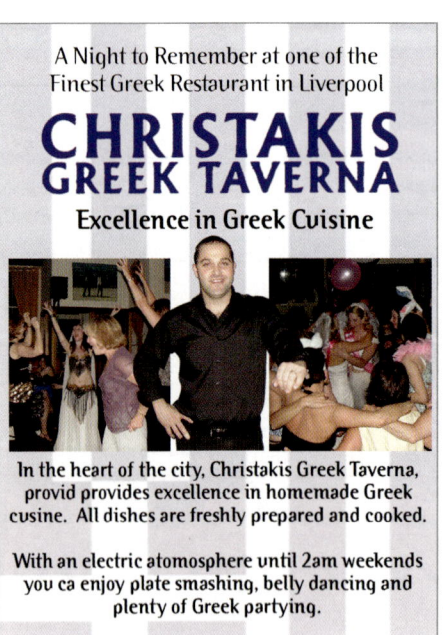

A Night to Remember at one of the Finest Greek Restaurant in Liverpool

CHRISTAKIS
GREEK TAVERNA
Excellence in Greek Cuisine

In the heart of the city, Christakis Greek Taverna, provid provides excellence in homemade Greek cusine. All dishes are freshly prepared and cooked.

With an electric atomosphere until 2am weekends you ca enjoy plate smashing, belly dancing and plenty of Greek partying.

7 York Street (Off Duke Street) Liverpool 1
Tel: (0151) 708 7377
www.christakisgreektaberna.com

Boasting a wide ranging menu from traditional breakfasts to tapas and A la Carte with a good vegetarian selection.

Expect a warm atmosphere, friendly attentive staff and mood enhancing surroundings.

'Hidden little gem...'
'minamalist yet friendly...'
'Top class, great staff'.
Liverpool Echo

Kinselas

72 Rose Lane (off Allerton Road) L18 8AG
Tel. 0151 724 6439

■ **Royal Consulate of Norway**
India Buildings, Water Street L1
Tel: (0151) 236 4871
■ **Consulate of Sweden**
Port of Liverpool Building,
Pier Head L1
Tel: (0151) 236 6666
■ **Royal Thai Consulate**
35 Lord Street L2
Tel: (0151) 255 0504

Faith

With 2004 designated as Liverpool's Year of Faith there's been increased interest in the churches, temples and places of worship that reflect the city's many religious communities. In the past churches serving the German, Greek, Italian, Polish and Swedish populations were established due to Liverpool's importance as a centre of shipping, and new arrivals have since expanded the diversity of faith within the city.

Afro Caribbean
■ **Merseyside Caribbean Community Centre**
1 Amberley Street
(near Women's Hospital) L8
Tel: (0151) 708 9790

Buddhism
■ **Buddhist Duldzin Centre**
25 Aigburth Drive L17
Tel: (0151) 726 8900
■ **Kagyu Shedrup Ling Tibetan Buddhist Centre**
15 Hawarden Avenue L17
Tel: (0151) 722 7649

Chinese
■ **Chinese Christian Disciples Church**
30 Hope Street L1
Tel: (0151) 709 4565
■ **Chinese Gospel Church**
19-20 Great George Square L1 5DY
Tel: (0151) 709 5050
■ **Pagoda Chinese Community Centre**
Henry Street L1
Tel: (0151) 708 8833

Christianity
■ **Anglican Cathedral**
6 Cathedral Close L1
Tel: (0151) 702 7217
■ **Diocese of Liverpool**
Church House, 1 Hanover Street L1
Tel: (0151) 708 9480
■ **Quaker Friends Meeting House**
65 Paradise Street L1
Tel: (0151) 708 6361
■ **Metropolitan Cathedral of Christ the King**
Mount Pleasant L3
Tel: (0151) 709 9222
■ **Roman Catholic Chaplaincy**
St Philip Neri Church
Catherine Street L8
Tel: (0151) 709 3858
■ **Seventh Day Adventist Church**
35 Kensington L7
Tel: (0151) 264 8044
■ **Unitarian Church**
57 Ullet Road L17 2AA
Tel: (0151) 733 1927

Hinduism
■ **Baha'i Centre**
1 Langdale Road
(off Smithdown Road) L15
Tel: (0151) 733 8614
■ **Hindu Cultural Organisation**
Edge Lane L7 5NA
Tel: (0151) 263 7965

Islam
■ **Ar-Rahma Mosque**
29-31 Hatherley Street L8
Tel: (0151) 709 7504
■ **Liverpool Mosque & Islamic Institute**
8 Cramond Avenue L18
Tel: (0151) 734 1222

Judaism
■ **Childwall Hebrew Congregation**
Dunbabin Road L15
Tel: (0151) 722 2979
■ **Liverpool Progressive Synagogue**
28 Church Road North L15
Tel: (0151) 733 5871

Sikhism
■ **Sikh Gurdwara Temple**
Wellington Avenue
Liverpool 15
Tel: (0151) 734 3022

Walks, tours and cruises

Combination tickets are available for some tours and attractions. Check individually or at the Tourist Information Centres where you can also make bookings. Call Tourist Hotline on 0906 680 6886 for full details (calls cost 25p per minute).

City Centre
■ **The Yellow Duckmarine**
Tel: (0151) 708 7799
Visit: theyellowduckmarine.co.uk
Hour-long land-and-river tour of waterfront, city and docks, on authentic WWII landing craft. Daily from 11am. £9.95 adult, £7.95 child (two to 15), £29 family, £8.95 concession, registered disabled,

211 Details

carer. Ticket entitles holder to £1 discount on The Beatles Story entrance. Ticket office and pick-up: Albert Dock. No wheelchair access.
■ **City Sightseeing Tour**
Tel: (0151) 933 2324
Hour-long open-top bus trip of city-centre with Blue Badge guide. Daily from 11am. £6 adult, £4.50 child (five to 15), £16 family, £4.50 senior citizen. Pick-up: The Beatles Story, Albert Dock. No wheelchair access
■ **Wingate Tours**
Tel: (0151) 547 2713
Explore the city-centre and Beatles sites with a guide. Caters for parties of up to 100 people.

Culture, Heritage & Wildlife
■ **Mersey Ferries River Explorer Cruise**
Tel: (0151) 630 1030
Visit: merseyferries.co.uk
Fifty-minute cruise on the Mersey for the best views of Liverpool's spectacular waterfront. Stop off at Seacombe Aquarium or Pirates Paradise, a play area for children. Mon-Fri 10am-3pm; Sat-Sun 10am-6pm every hour. £2.30 single/4.50 return adult, £1.30, £2.50 child (five to 15), £11.70 family, £1.80, £3.30 concession. Combined tickets available for cruise and Aquarium Departs: Pier Head.
■ **Special Cruises on the River**
Throughout the year there are themed river trips: Liverbird Wildlife Discovery, Liverpool Bay, Caribbean Evening, Beatles, 1960s, Glam Rock, Halloween

and Fireworks and Children's Xmas Cruises. Call above for details and schedule.
■ **Central Library Tour**
Tel: (0151) 233 5844
The second floor of the Central Library on William Brown Street has a fine book collection open to the public. Guided tours on second Tuesday of each month from 2.15pm.
■ **Sandon Dock Visitor Centre**
Regent Road, Bootle
Tel: 01925 233 233
Visit: nww.co.uk
Down the plug but where does it go? What actually happens when the water goes down the drain? Come and see inside a wastewater treatment works. Guided tours by appointment. Mon-Fri. Free.
■ **Liverpool Heritage Cab City Tours**
Tel: (0151) 531 6947
Experience the city's history in a taxi or 1920s-style car-hire tour.
■ **Radio City Tower**
Tel: (0151) 709 3285
Visit: radiocity.co.uk
Guided tours around one of the city's most unusual buildings – and unbeatable views. Sat-Sun £5 adult, £2.50 concession. Limited disabled access, lift.
■ **Liverpool Pub Culture Tour**
Tel: (0151) 928 6691
or: 07968 528505
■ **Joseph Williamson Tunnels**
Smithdown Lane L7
Tel: (0151) 709 6868
Visit: williamsontunnels.co.uk
What lies beneath? A fascinating underground network of tunnels, built in the 19th Century, plus exhibitions depicting the life and times of the eccentric who built them. Apr-Oct: Tue-Sun 10am-5pm. Oct-Mar: Thu-Sun 10am-4pm. £3.50 adult, £2 child, £5 family, £3 concession. Very limited disabled access.
■ **Cains Brewery**
Stanhope Street L8
Tel: (0151) 709 8734

Visit: cainsbeer.com
Victorian brewery producing award-winning tours including buffet and two pints in Brewery Tap pub. Mon-Thu 6.30pm-8pm. £3.75 over 18s only.

Walks
■ **City Walks**
Tel: (0151) 652 3692
Explore the city's architecture and art on foot with a Blue Badge guide. May-Sept. Departs: Tourist Information Centre, Queen Square.
■ **Sunday City Walks**
Tel: (0151) 928 0630
Weekly walking tours with Blue Badge guide. Sun 2pm. Departure: Tourist Information Centre, Queen Sq.
■ **Albert Dock & Waterfront Walk**
Tel: (0151) 336 1818
Take in the stories and buildings of the historic waterfront on a 90-minute exploration with a qualified guide. Thu-Sat 11.15am & 2pm. £3 adult, £2 under16s and senior citizens. Departs: Gower Street, Albert Dock
■ **Slavery History Trail**
Tel: (0151) 726 0941
Guided tours of areas connected to Liverpool's slave trade. Sat-Sun 11am. £2.50 adult, £1.50 under16s and senior citizens.
■ **Mersey Tourism Blue Badge**
Tel: (0151) 237 3925
Over 30 Blue Badge guides available for car, coach and walking tours. Foreign language guides on request, plus 12-seater mini bus hire.

Portia World Travel

6 North John Street • Liverpool L2 4SD

Specialists in:
- Low cost flights • Tailor made holidays
- Independent travel arrangements
- Long haul and cruises • Package holidays

Tel. 0151 227 3401   Fax. 0151 227 1176
Email: leisure@pwt.mersinet.co.uk

Q'DOS
HAIR COLOUR SPECIALISTS

183 Park Road,
Liverpool L8 6SE
Tel. 0151 728 9932

- Holders of Wella Master in colour award
- Crisp, fresh, city centre styling
- Student discounts
- Thursday late night

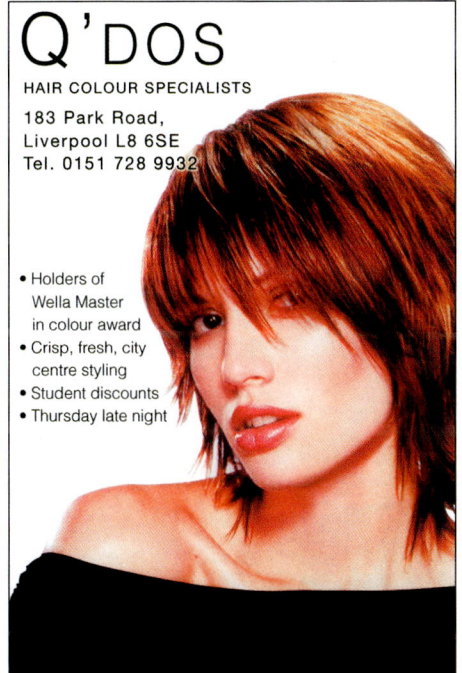

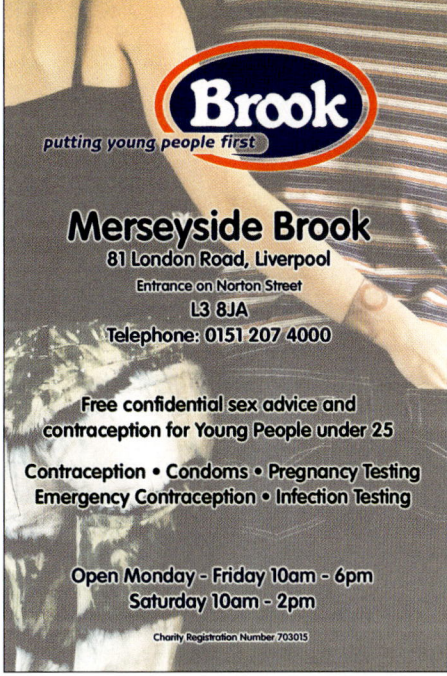

Brook
putting young people first

Merseyside Brook
81 London Road, Liverpool
Entrance on Norton Street
L3 8JA
Telephone: 0151 207 4000

Free confidential sex advice and contraception for Young People under 25

Contraception • Condoms • Pregnancy Testing
Emergency Contraception • Infection Testing

Open Monday - Friday 10am - 6pm
Saturday 10am - 2pm

Charity Registration Number 703015

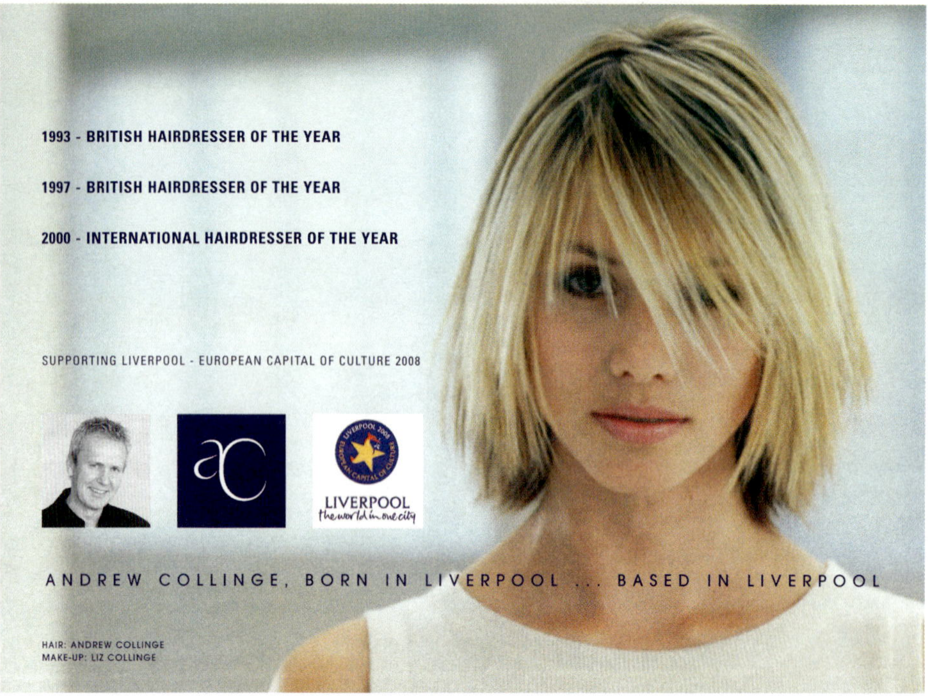
1993 - BRITISH HAIRDRESSER OF THE YEAR
1997 - BRITISH HAIRDRESSER OF THE YEAR
2000 - INTERNATIONAL HAIRDRESSER OF THE YEAR
SUPPORTING LIVERPOOL - EUROPEAN CAPITAL OF CULTURE 2008
LIVERPOOL
the world in one city
ANDREW COLLINGE, BORN IN LIVERPOOL ... BASED IN LIVERPOOL
HAIR: ANDREW COLLINGE
MAKE-UP: LIZ COLLINGE

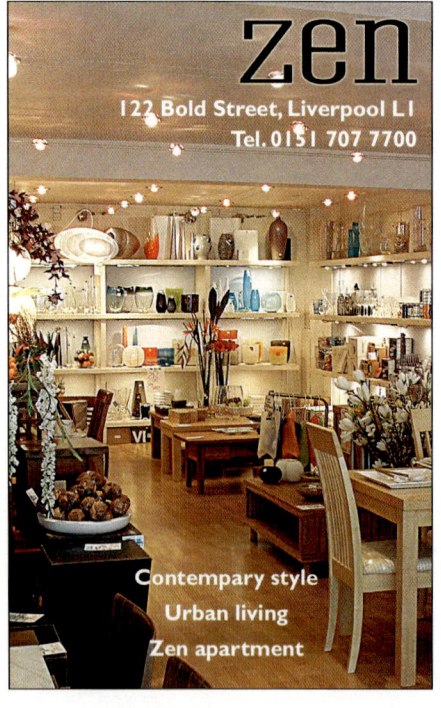

zen
122 Bold Street, Liverpool L1
Tel. 0151 707 7700
Contempary style
Urban living
Zen apartment

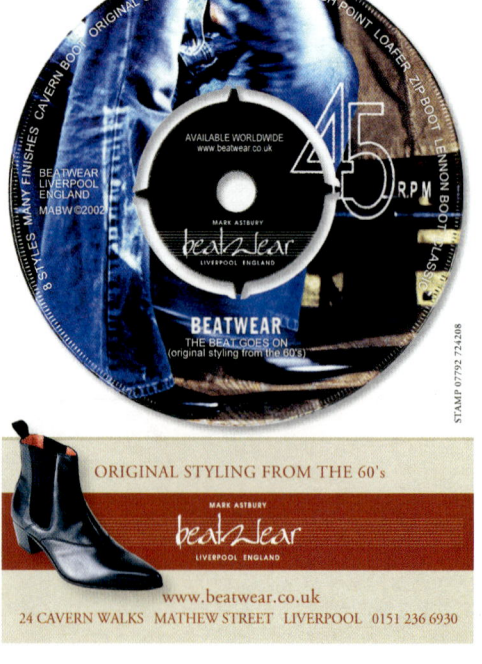

8 STYLES MANY FINISHES CAVERN BOOT ORIGINAL CHELSEA WINKLE PICKER HIGH POINT LOAFER ZIP BOOT LENNON BOOT CLASSIC
AVAILABLE WORLDWIDE
www.beatwear.co.uk
BEATWEAR
LIVERPOOL
ENGLAND
MABW ©2002
45
R.P.M
MARK ASTBURY
beatwear
LIVERPOOL ENGLAND
BEATWEAR
THE BEAT GOES ON
(original styling from the 60's)
ORIGINAL STYLING FROM THE 60's
MARK ASTBURY
beatwear
LIVERPOOL ENGLAND
www.beatwear.co.uk
24 CAVERN WALKS MATHEW STREET LIVERPOOL 0151 236 6930

STAMP 07792 724208

The following guides have specialist knowledge:

■ Sylvia McMurty
Tel: (0151) 709 9313
or: 0771 500 2464
(Beatles and Liverpool car, coach, minibus and walking tours day and evening).

■ Hilary Oxlade
Tel: (0151) 931 3075
or: 07803 206 599
(ar and minibus tours of Liverpool and Northwest, plus Beatles).

■ Phil Coppell
Tel: (0151) 920 7568
or: 07710 507 656
(professional guiding service for city, sport, media and Beatles).

■ Phil Hughes
Tel: (0151) 228 4565
or: 07961 511 223
(German-speaking guide for ale trails and sports tours).

■ Jerry Williams
Tel: (0151) 608 3769
(Merseyside and the American Civil War).

Beatles tours

■ The Beatles Story
Britannia Vaults, Albert Dock
Tel: (0151) 709 1963
Visit: beatlesstory.com
Relive the rise of the band from the Cavern to Beatlemania. The complete Fab Four experience.
Daily Apr-Sept 10am-6pm; Oct-Mar 10am-4pm. £7.95 adult, £4.95 child, £23 family, £4.45 concession. Fully accessible.

■ Magical Mystery Tour
Tel: (0151) 709 3285
or: 0871 222 1963
Visit: cavern-liverpool.co.uk
Two-hour tour starts at the Beatles Story and ends at the Cavern Club on Mathew Street, taking in all Fab Four references along the way. Daily. £10.95. Departs: 2.10pm Queen Square, 2.30pm The Beatles Story, Albert Dock. Extra tours throughout year, call to check.
No wheelchair access.

■ Cavern City Tours
Specialised Beatles tours and weekend packages, including International Beatles Week in August.
No wheelchair access.
Contact as above.

■ Live@pool Tours
Tel: (0151) 330 0844
Visit: liveapool.com
Themed coach tours. In English, call Jackie Spencer on 07990 761478; Japanese, Shuji Tohyama on 07867 627362

■ Mendips and 20 Forthlin Road
Tel: (0151) 708 8574 (morning tours)
or: (0151) 427 7231 (afternoon tours)
Visit: spekehall.org.uk
The childhood homes of John Lennon and Paul McCartney respectively. These are National Trust properties, visits are only available with organised tours. 27 Mar-31 Oct, Wed-Sun. £12 National Trust members, £6 non-members, accompanied children free. Departs: 10.30am & 11.20am Albert Dock; 2.15pm & 3.55pm Speke Hall.

■ Beatles Car Tours
Call to arrange a personalised trip with guide:
Sylvia McMurtry on (0151) 709 9313 and Hilary Oxlade on (0151) 931 3075

■ Takuji Abe
Tel: (0151) 220 9543
Japanese-speaking Beatles guide.

Other Beatles attractions

■ Beatles Shop
31 Mathew Street L2
Tel: (0151) 236 8066

■ Cavern Club
Mathew Street L2
Tel: (0151) 236 1965

■ Cavern Pub
Mathew Street L2
Tel: (0151) 236 4041
Visit: cavern-liverpool.co.uk

■ From Me To You
Cavern Walks, Mathew Street L2
Tel: (0151) 227 1963
Visit: beatles64.co.uk

■ Mathew Street Gallery
Mathew Street L2
Tel: (0151) 236 0009
Exhibition of John Lennon's art and Beatles photos with limited-edition prints for sale.

Sport

■ Aintree Racecourse & The Grand National Experience
Ormskirk Road, Aintree L9
Tel: (0151) 522 2921
Visit: aintree.co.uk
Experience the wonder of the world-famous Grand National steeplechase racecourse and its sumptuous facilities. Includes a trip on the Grand National simulator, tour of the legendary course, stables, weighing room and visit to the mythical Red Rum's grave and Aintree Museum. Twice a day, 22 May-21 Oct.

215 **Details**

Site seeing
Where to find Liverpool on the www…

Photography
- simonjones.co.uk/photography
Local snapper's gallery of Quick Time movies, including 360-degree panoramic views from the Pier Head and the top of the Royal Liver Building.
- liverpoolphotography.co.uk
Great aerial shots by Simon Kirwan, former Observer Outdoor Photographer of the Year whose images have appeared in many books and magazines.
- liverpoolphotos.com
Epic skyscapes by Guy Woodland, photographer from Liverpool: The First 1,000 Years (see recommended reading). This is his online picture library.
- liverpoolpictorial.co.uk
Fabbest of the fab, categorised by postcode with some wonderful shots of the gritty docklands. Check out those marine dredgers!

Culture and heritage
- liverpoolculture.com
Official site celebrating the 2008 European Capital of Culture title and reporting on the hundreds of projects planned and underway for the greatest show on earth.
- liverpoolarchitecture.com
Joint-venture by the University and Liverpool Architecture Society, with online tours of the best buildings in the Business District.
- mersey-gateway.org
A huge project that will eventually incorporate 20,000 digital images illustrating the history and growth of the port of Liverpool.
- lmu.livjm.ac.uk/etms
Unique database of Liverpool life compiled by John Moores University, with photographs and artefacts from the last eight centuries.

- liverpoolhistorysociety.org.uk
Online forum for local historians and anyone with a story to tell. They also publish a regular newsletter and annual journal.
- merseymouth.com
Prose and poetry, whimsy and nostalgia. From the hottest nightclub in 70s Liverpool to the quest for a docker's overcoat.

Regeneration
- liverpoolvision.com
Documenting the city's fast-paced renaissance under the Strategic Regeneration Framework produced by public and private sectors.
- liverpool2007.org.uk
Gateway to the city's historic past plus an insight into the forces that are shaping modern Liverpool in the run-up to its 800th anniversary.
- liverpoolfourthgrace.co.uk
Information and downloads about the iconic – and controversial – new development on the waterfront, 'an architectural signature that will be read by the world'.

General information
- visitliverpool.com
Official tourism site created by The Mersey Partnership. Arts and culture, sport and entertainment, events and attractions.
- liverpool.gov.uk
The Council's official site. Everything you ever wanted to know about how the city of Liverpool is run, with a comprehensive A-Z section.
- bbc.co.uk/liverpool
Excellent local coverage from the Beeb with news and listings, a webcam updated every five minutes and lively expats forum.

- icliverpool.com
Online version of the Liverpool Daily Post & Echo packed with up-to-the-minute information and some handy restaurant reviews.
- merseyguide.co.uk
'To bring you the information you need to explore and enjoy the county of Merseyside'. Visitors can subscribe to a newsletter.
- seeliverpool.com
40 pages of information and more than 70 links, with suggested sightseeing schedules and a concise guide for Beatles fans.

Football (unofficial)
- bluekipper.com
Virulent and vociferous Everton FC fan site, with a great section on funnies overheard at the match. Warning: the language can be choice.
- raotl.co.uk
Web version of the Liverpool FC fanzine, Red All Over The Land. All the Kopite banter, no shortage of opinion and some cracking T-shirts for sale.
- shankly.com
Online shrine to the legendary Liverpool FC manager and one of the city's greatest adopted sons. "The problem with you, son, is that your brains are all in your head…"

Details 216

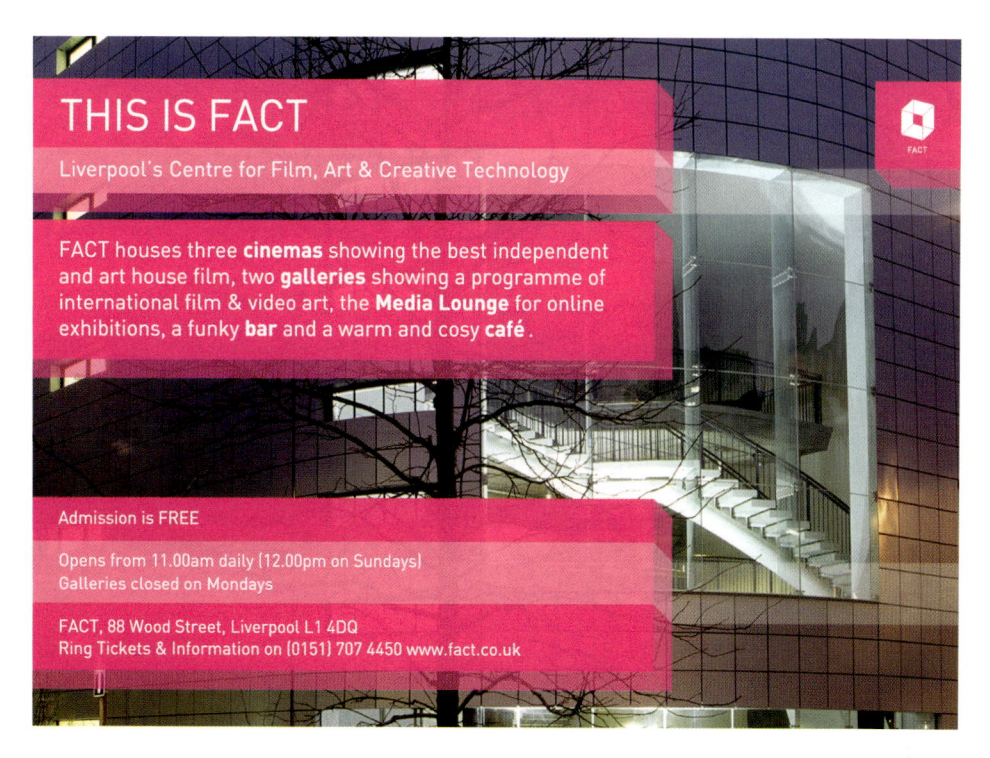

THIS IS FACT

Liverpool's Centre for Film, Art & Creative Technology

FACT houses three **cinemas** showing the best independent and art house film, two **galleries** showing a programme of international film & video art, the **Media Lounge** for online exhibitions, a funky **bar** and a warm and cosy **café**.

Admission is FREE

Opens from 11.00am daily (12.00pm on Sundays)
Galleries closed on Mondays

FACT, 88 Wood Street, Liverpool L1 4DQ
Ring Tickets & Information on (0151) 707 4450 www.fact.co.uk

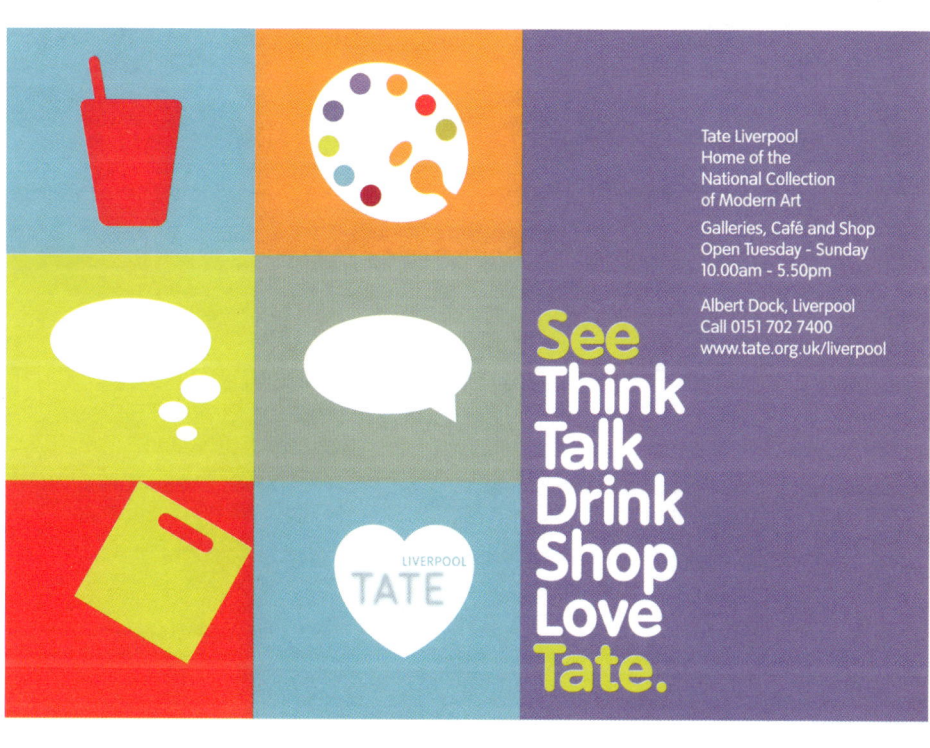

Tate Liverpool
Home of the
National Collection
of Modern Art

Galleries, Café and Shop
Open Tuesday - Sunday
10.00am - 5.50pm

Albert Dock, Liverpool
Call 0151 702 7400
www.tate.org.uk/liverpool

**See
Think
Talk
Drink
Shop
Love
Tate.**

■ **Everton FC Tour**
Goodison Park L4
Tel: **(0151) 330 2277**
Visit: **evertonfc.com**
Award-winning tour that lasts for over one hour and can accommodate individuals, small parties and large groups (with optional two-course meal). Mon, Wed and Fri: 11am & 2pm. £6.50 adult, £4.50 children/ over 65s, £18 family.
Strictly advance booking.

■ **Liverpool FC Museum & Tour Centre**
Anfield Road L4
Tel: **(0151) 260 6677**
Visit: **liverpoolfc.tv**
Home of England's most successful football club. Highlights in the museum include four huge European Cups, a 60-seat cinema and re-creation of the famous standing Spion Kop. Don't forget to touch the 'This Is Anfield' sign by the players tunnel. Every weekday 10am-5pm (hour before kick-off on matchdays). Museum & Tour: £9 adults £9.00, £5.50 children/OAPS, family £23. Museum only: £5 adults £5.00, £3 children/OAPS, £13 families. Strictly advance booking.

TV and radio
■ BBC North West and Granada (part of the ITV network) broadcast regular news bulletins throughout the day on terrestrial TV as well airing a variety of regional programmes. The main radio stations are BBC Radio Merseyside (95.8FM), Radio City 96.7 and 107.6 Juice FM.

Newspapers and magazines
■ **Liverpool Daily Post & Echo**
Morning and evening sister newspapers established in the city for almost 200 years. The Post has a long history of progressive liberalism, while the Echo is an institution among ordinary Liverpudlians. Published daily, Mon-Sat (the Football Echo, published Saturdays during the football season, provides the latest news and action from the region's teams).
■ **Space**
The city's premier lifestyle magazine. Bi-monthly. Free.
■ **Your Move**
Essential property magazine. Fortnightly. Free.
■ **Live Magazine**
Listings for all live performances. Every six weeks. Free.
■ **The Evertonian**
Official magazine of Everton FC. Monthly.

■ **LFC Magazine**
Official magazine of Liverpool FC. Weekly.
■ **The Kop**
News and gossip for Liverpool FC fanatics. Monthly.

Colleges and universities
■ **European Languages Centre**
Northern House,
43-45 Pembroke Place L3
Tel: **(0151) 708 7071**
Visit: **eurolang.com**
English language school for visitors. Also offers most European languages including Japanese, Turkish, Russian and Chinese dialects.
■ **Liverpool Community College**
Tel: **(0151) 252 3000**
Visit: **liv-coll.ac.uk**
Four brand new buildings in the city centre and courses from performing arts to travel and tourism to fashion and clothing.
■ **Liverpool Institute of Performing Arts**
Mount Street L1
Tel: **(0151) 330 3000**
Visit: **lipa.ac.uk**
LIPA is regarded as one of the country's outstanding fame academies. Paul McCartney is the leading patron, and it's devoted to providing excellent learning programmes and resources for budding actors, dancers, musicians, technicians, managers and designers.
■ **University of Liverpool**
Tel: **(0151) 794 2000**
Visit: **liv.ac.uk**
One of the UK's leading universities, renowned for its world-class teaching and research excellence. Six faculties, eight Nobel Laureates, 54 departments and schools, nearly 3,000 international students and over 400 industry partners.
■ **Liverpool John Moores University**
Tel: **(0151) 231 2121**
Visit: **livjm.ac.uk**
One of Merseyside's greatest assets, with an influence and presence stretching far further than the city boundaries. Boasts 20,000 students and 2,500 staff.

Clubs and societies
■ **Artists Club**
5 Eberle Street L2
Tel: **(0151) 236 2940**
Opulent surroundings just off Dale Street, opposite Garlands nightclub and behind an unassuming blue door. In existence since 1877 and now primarily a gentleman's lunching club.

Details 218

■ **Athenaeum**
Church Alley L3
Tel: **(0151) 709 7770**
A nationally-renowned library, top-class dining room and meeting room, housed in an elegant building off Church Street near Bluecoat Chambers. The original club was established way back in 1797 to provide a meeting place where ideas and information could be exchanged (its early proprietors played a major part in the movement to end slavery).

■ **Duncan Society**
**Dept of Sociology,
University of Liverpool,
Eleanor Rathbone Building,
Bedford Street South L69**
Tel: **(0151) 794 2986**
Visit: **duncansociety.org.uk**
Named after the city's pioneering 19th century Medical Officer. Conceived to stimulate debate, discussion and understanding on contemporary health issues. Open to all.

■ **Liverpool Yemeni Arabic Club**
167a Lodge Lane L8
Tel: **(0151) 734 0550**
Or LYAC for short, working alongside Yemeni-speaking people in the city and those interested in Arabic culture.

■ **Marina & Harbourside Club**
Coburg Wharf, Sefton Street L3
Tel: **(0151) 709 7770**
Visit: **liverpoolmarina.com**
Sailing club with an urban feel and excellent location overlooking the River Mersey. Fully licensed with conference facilities and a great place for Sunday lunch.

■ **Merseyside Inter-Faith Group**
Tel: **(0151) 733 1541**
Multi-denominational meetings once a month at different venues for faith-sharing, learning and mutual enrichment. Anyone is welcome to come along.

■ **Racquet Club**
**Hargreaves Buildings,
5 Chapel Street L3**
Tel: **(0151) 236 6676**
Visit: **raquetclub.co.uk**
Since transformed into an elegant boutique hotel near the waterfront, it still plays host to a sporting club founded back in 1874, with lovely reception rooms and bars.

Kids stuff...

■ Liverpool Museum's hands-on **Natural History Centre & Planetarium**, with shows specially-created for different age-groups...
■ Five-mile safari through 450 acres of parkland at **Knowsley Safari Park**...
■ One-hour tour of Liverpool's historic waterfront, starting at **Albert Dock**...
■ Central Library's **Mystery Children's Centre** with Sensory Room where kids with emotional problems can 'chill out' in a magical aquatic kingdom...
■ **Yellow Duckmarine,** in and out of the water...
■ Mummified Egyptian crocodile at **Conservation Centre**...
■ Smuggling stories at **Merseyside Maritime Museum,** plus the sights and sounds of emigration...
■ **Hollywood Bowl** at Edge Lane Retail Park, just outside city-centre...
■ Time machine at **International Space & Astronomy Centre (ISAC)** by Seacombe Ferry Terminal...
■ Puppets, costumes and picture trails at the **Walker's Artbase** every weekend and daily from 19 July to 5 Sept for the school holidays...

219 Details

International Inn
★ ★ ★ *Independent Hostel*

Welcome to the...

★ Award winning tourist hostel in a prime city centre location in the heart of Liverpool. Former Victorian warehouse, full of character with modern facilities, excelling in customer service and information.

★ Dormitories all en-suite for 2, 4, 6, 8 and 10. Clean bedding, TV lounge, internet café, kitchen, no curfew, 24hrs access.

★ Beds from £15ppn Twin rooms from £36 per room per night.

FREE TEA, COFFEE & TOAST ALL DAY, EVERY DAY

✆ +(44) 0151 709 8135
4 South Hunter Street (Off Hardman Street)
Liverpool City Centre
www.internationalinn.co.uk
info@internationalinn.co.uk

Winner - Mersey Tourism Awards, Outstanding Customer Service 2004
Nominated - Mersey Tourism Awards, Small Tourism Business 2004
Shortlisted - Academy Ambassador Award for Excellence in Customer Care 2002
Winner - Academy Ambassador award for Excellence in Customer Care
Winner - Mersey Tourism Best Customer Service
Winner - Mersey Tourism Awards, Small Tourism Business 2002

Maggie Mays
CAFE BAR

Expect a warm welcome and friendly service in this family run business.

Established for 10 years, Maggie Mays provides a relaxed atmosphere in the heart of the City Centre of Liverpool. Serving traditional meals all day, every day. Daily specials available.

Traditional Foods ~ Disabled access
Baby changing
Open Mon–Fri 9.30 – 7pm
Saturday 9.30 – 6pm ~ Sunday 10.30

90 Bold Street, Liverpool L1 4HY
Tel. 0151 709 7600

Index

Abercromby Square 59, 102, 173
Adelphi Hotel 73, 94, 111
African Oye Festival 14
Aintree 6, 190, 215
Albert Dock 8, 13, 14, 31, 32, 36, 49, 56, 109, 142, 153, 163, 212
Albion House 23, 58, 60
Alsop, Will 16, 36, 53
Aluna Project 36
Anderson's Bar 22, 59, 143
Anfield 94, 191
Anglican Cathedral 24, 44, 90, 96-97, 98, 211
Architecture 17-27, 208
Armani 6, 153, 158, 159
Art Deco 18, 20, 54, 57, 45, 174, 188
Athenaeum 66, 70-71, 219
Aubudon, John James 102, 171, 173

Baby Cream 50, 131, 142
Baltic Fleet 142, 176
Bang & Olufsen 59, 163
Bank of England 58, 62
Banks 200
Beatles 8, 16, 64, 65, 67, 109, 111, 146, 150, 169, 172, 188, 215
Beatles Cruise 14
Beatles Shop 67
Beatles Story 8, 50, 215
Beetham Plaza 6, 101, 174
Beetham Tower 6, 30, 58, 59, 176
Biennial 6, 13, 16, 176
Big Top Tent 16
Bilbao 31
Birthday, 800th 16, 73
Blue Badge Guides 212
Blue Bar & Grill 50, 131, 142
Bluecoat Arts/Display Centre 69, 163, 171, 208

Bluecoat Chambers 66, 69
Bluecoat Courtyard 44
Blue Funnel Line 84, 104
Bluu 148
Bold Street 26, 83, 84, 85, 91
Boodle & Dunthorne 59, 162
Boston 79
Brunswick Dock 31, 35, 36
Bryson, Bill 10
Buffalo Bill 10
Bulloch, James 60
Business District 13, 23, 26, 46, 57-64, 143
Butch Cassidy 10

Calderstones Park 16, 39, 192
Canada Dock 34, 103
Canals 31, 36
Canning Dock 14, 56
Canning Street 99, 105
Carling Academy 76, 188
Castle Street 20, 23, 26, 57, 117
Catharine Street 100, 106
Cathedrals 6
Cavern, The 8, 67, 188
Cavern Walks 66, 67, 153, 156
Central Docks 32, 36
Central Library 16, 23, 76, 77, 93, 102, 171, 212
Chambre-Hardman House 90, 93
Chapel Street 23, 57, 103, 117
Chavasse Park 39, 73, 115, 163
Chicago 51
Chinatown 83, 84, 104, 134
Chinese Arch 84
Chinese New Year 14
Christmas Cruise 14
Christmas Lights 13, 16
Church Street 65, 67, 68, 73
Cities at the Edge Festival 31
City Council 207
City Exchange 58, 150
City of Light 16

City Sightseeing 8, 212
Classic Films at the Phil 14, 181
Clayton Square 67, 153
Coat of Arms 10, 18
Coburg Dock 31
Collingwood Dock 34
Columbus, Christopher 43
Comedy 6, 186
Compton House 18, 68
Conran, Terence 163
Conservation Areas 32, 75, 99
Conservation Centre 66, 79, 166
Consulates 207
Cormorant 10
Cossons, Sir Neil 10
Cotton Exchange 10, 24, 58, 59
County Sessions House 13, 76, 79
Cream 85, 148
Creamfields 6, 13, 16
Cricket 157, 161
Crowne Plaza 14, 31, 36, 50, 51, 115
Croxteth Hall 39
Cruise-liner terminal 6, 16, 31
CUBE 88, 171
Cultural Quarter 23, 44, 46, 75-82, 146
Cunard 13, 52, 56
Cunard Building 49, 50, 52

Dale Street 23
Dickens, Charles 73, 94, 148
Dingle 32
Dock Wall 32, 33
Drome 157, 161
Duke's Terrace 6, 87
Duke Street 83, 85
Duncan, Dr William 93, 146
29, 208

221 Index

East Village 6, 84, 86
Eleanor Rigby 8, 67
Elmes, Harvey Lonsdale 62, 80
Emergency Services 204
Empire Theatre 75, 76, 181
Engine Room Monument 50
English Heritage 10, 39
Est Est Est 50, 132
European Capital of Culture 6, 16, 156, 165
European Market 13, 14, 16, 163
Everton Football Club 190, 216, 218
Everyman Theatre 90, 182
Exchange Flags 64
Exchange Street East 22

FACT 6, 16, 84, 88, 172
Fashion 6, 160-161
Festival of Light 13
Filini 126
Films 6
Fireworks Cruise 14
Fireworks Display 13, 16
Food & Drink Festival 13, 16
Football 6
Formby Point 196
Forthlin Road 8, 215
Foster, John 97
Fourth Grace 6, 16, 31, 49, 50, 53, 54, 216
Fury, Billy 169

Garlands 6, 143
George's Dock Building 50, 54-55, 62
Gerrard, Steven 191
Gibson, John 49, 169
Gladstone, William 82, 90, 93, 100
Golf 6, 192
Graces, Three 53, 49

Grand Central Auditorium 90, 134
Grand National 14, 16, 161, 189, 190, 215
Grapes, The 8, 9, 146
Great Escape, The 69, 174
Greek Revival 18, 85
Guided tours 211
Gyms 194

Hargreaves Building 23, 103
Hartley, Jesse 56
Hawthorne, Nathaniel 32
Haymarket 23
Heathcliff 8
Helplines 207
Hemingways 84, 176
Heritage Open Days 13, 16, 79
Historic Warships 197
Hope Quarter 46, 51, 89-100, 123, 141, 150
Hope Street Hotel 6, 112, 124
Hope Street Midsummer Festival 14
Horrocks, Jeremiah 9
Hospitals 204
Hotels 6, 109-119
HUB Festival 16

India Building 62
International Beatles Week 13, 16
International Guitar Festival 16
Irish 34, 91, 146, 203
Isaacs, Jeremy 165

Jacaranda 8, 84, 148
James Street 23, 57
Jewish Heritage Trail 105
John Lennon Airport 6, 203
John Moores University 8, 14, 218
JMU Fashion Show 14

Juice FM 151, 218
Jung, Carl 9

Kidd, Jodie 10
King's Dock 31, 36
King's Waterfront 6, 16
Kop, Spion 191, 218
Knowsley Safari Park 196, 219

Lantern Festival 13, 16
La's, The 9
Lennon, Cynthia 66
Lennon, John 8, 9, 67, 145, 148
Lever Gallery 72, 167
Lewisohn, Mark 8
Lime Street 75, 76, 111
LIPA 6, 90, 181, 218
Listed properties 18, 83
Liver Birds 6, 23, 51, 76, 100, 117, 146
Liverpool Arabic Arts Festival 16
Liverpool Art School 14
Liverpool Bay Cruise 14
Liverpool Bird Wildlife Discovery 14
Liverpool Daily Post & Echo 58, 216, 218
Liverpool Echo 13
Liverpool Echo Entertainment Awards 16
Liverpool Echo Fashion Show 13, 16
Liverpool Festival of Comedy 16
Liverpool Football Club 10, 67, 160, 191, 216, 218
Liverpool International Tennis Tournament 16, 39
Liverpool Irish Festival 13, 16
Liverpool Marina 6, 31, 35, 193, 219
Liverpool Museum 76, 77, 167
Liverpool Palace 161
Liverpool Perfoming Arts Festival 14
Liverpool Resurgent 73
Liverpool Triathalon 13, 16
Liverpool Vision 7
Liverpool Women's 10k Run 14, 39

Index 222

Liverpool Yacht Club 193
Living Room, The 59, 131, 143
London Carriage Works 91, 112, 124
Lord Mayor's Parade 14
Lord Street 14
Lusitania 50, 51, 56, 167
Lyceum 26, 85

Magnet, The 91
Markets 163
Marseille 31
Martins Banks 24, 58, 62, 63
Mathew Street 8, 9, 66, 67, 128, 172
Mathew Street Festival 13
McCartney, Paul 8, 39, 181, 208
Melville, Herman 31, 34, 73, 208
Memphis 6, 13
Mendips 8, 215
Mersey 24, 29, 31, 34, 59, 60, 61
Mersey Docks & Harbour Company 53
Mersey Ferries 8, 30, 203, 204, 212
Mersey River Festival 14, 16, 34
Merseyside Jazz Festival 14
Merseyside Maritime Museum 50, 56, 167
Merseysippi Jazz Band 14
Mersey Waterfront Regional Park 36
Met Quarter 6, 153
Metropolitan Cathedral 90, 95, 211
Mississippi 9
Museum of Liverpool Life 50, 56, 104, 168, 169

Naples 31
National Museums Liverpool 166-170
National Trust 93
National Wildflower Centre 39, 196
Nelson Street 84, 104
Neptune 10, 24, 31, 51, 79
Neptune Theatre 66, 182
New Brighton 94, 197
Newington 6
Newsham Park 39

New Year's Eve Fireworks Display 13, 16
New York 10, 24, 31, 56, 73, 77, 97, 98, 102, 149
Newz Bar 6, 59, 131, 144, 176
Nook, The 84
North John Street 58, 67

Observatory 7, 66
Ocean 50
Old Hall Street 57, 174
Open Golf Championship 16, 192
Oratory 13, 97
Owen, Michael 191

Pacific Bar & Grill 59, 131, 144
Pall Mall 7
Palm House 40, 43, 150
Pan American Bar 7, 136, 142
Paradise Street 7, 39, 73, 153
Parish Church 58, 59
Parks and gardens 37-44
Parliament Street 39
Parr Street (3345) 84, 86, 128, 149
Penelope 7, 85, 176
Philharmonic Hall 10, 14, 62, 90, 94, 181
Philharmonic Hotel 51, 91, 92, 150, 174
Piazza Waterfall 101, 174, 176
Picasso, Pablo 24
Picton, James 22
Pier Head 13, 26, 30, 31, 36, 46, 49-56, 114, 142
Playhouse Theatre 66, 73, 93, 182
Portland Stone 26, 60
Port of Liverpool Building 24, 26, 49, 50, 53
Post Offices 200
Pre-Raphaelites 169, 170, 174
Prince's Dock 31, 49, 51
Probe Records 159, 160

Queen's Dock 31
Queen Square 66, 73, 123, 141
Queensway Tunnel 23, 34, 76
Queen Victoria 43, 64, 80

Racquet Club 7, 23, 58, 103, 114, 117, 125, 176, 219
Radisson SAS 6, 58, 109, 114, 116, 126, 127, 145
Rattle, Simon 10
Renshaw Street 91
RIBA 88
Rodney Street 92, 93
Room Store 50, 163
Rooney, Wayne 190
Rope Walks 7, 46, 83-88, 109, 123, 141, 147
Roscoe, William 91, 150
Round the World Clipper Race 16, 31
Rowse, Herbert 26, 54, 62, 76, 94
Royal Birkdale Golf Club 16, 192
Royal Court Theatre 188
Royal Liver Building 24, 25, 30, 36, 49, 50-51, 53, 92, 115, 146, 150
Royal Liverpool Golf Club 192
Royal Liverpool Philharmonic Orchestra 10, 181
Rumford Place 58, 60
Run Liverpool 13, 16

St Andrew's Church 90, 92
St Bride, Church of 21
St George's Hall 10, 18, 44, 62, 75, 76, 77, 80, 94
St James Cemetery 90, 98
St James Gardens 44
St John's Beacon 66, 72
St John's Gardens 44, 76, 82
St Luke's Church 90, 91

223 Index

St Petersburg 139
Salthouse Dock 14, 56
Sanctuary Stone 58, 64
Sandon Dock 33
Sapporo Teppanyaki 7, 86, 134
Scouse 8, 9, 186
Seacombe 30, 197
Seaforth 32, 34
Sefton Park 39, 40, 118, 174
Shanghai 31, 84
Shankly, Bill 190, 216
Shopping 7, 153-163
Shopping Centre 44, 46, 65-73, 146, 153
Simply Heathcotes 59, 125
Slavery Remembrance Day 13, 16
Society 84, 149
Southport 16, 36, 196
Southport Airshow 13, 16
Southport Flower Show 13, 16
Southport Jazz Festival 14
Spanish Garden 100
Spas 7
Stanley Dock 32
Stanley Hall 20, 58
Stanley Park 39
Steble Fountain 79
Streisand, Barbra 8
Sudley House 166, 169, 170
Summer Pops 16
Sundance Kid 10
SuperLambBanana 176
Sushi 7
Synagogue 105

Tall Ships 16, 31
Tate Liverpool 7, 50, 56, 173
Tatler 160
Tea Factory 84, 88, 124, 149, 171
Tennis 16, 39, 192
Thomas, Walter Aubrey 24, 51, 92
Titanic 60, 94, 111, 167
Tithebarn Street 24, 57
Tobacco Warehouse 32
Tourist Information Centres 8, 200
Town Hall 26, 58, 64
Toxteth 9, 60, 104

Trams 7, 31
Tunnels, Mersey 23, 34, 54
Twain, Mark 64

Ullet Road 91, 174, 211
UNESCO 7, 16, 31
Unitarian 91, 174, 211
United States 32, 51, 56, 60, 102, 132
Unity Theatre 7, 90, 182
University of Liverpool 100, 173, 218
Utility 163

Ventilation shafts 26, 27, 58
Victoria Street 23, 117, 141
Vines, The 11, 146, 150
Vivienne Westwood 6, 66, 67, 154-156, 160, 161

Wade Smith 158, 159
Walker Art Gallery 20, 49, 76, 79, 169
Wall of Fame 67
Wapping Dock 31
Warrington Wood, John 79, 166
Waterfront 29-36, 208
Waterfront Classics 13, 16
Waterfront Weekend 13
Waterloo Dock 32
Water Street 20, 23, 24, 57
Websites 216
Wellington's Column 20, 76, 81
White, Dave 8
White Star Line 23, 60, 146
William Brown Street 16, 20, 23, 75, 76, 77, 171, 181
Williamson Square 66, 73
Williamson Tunnels 7, 212
Wirral 30, 36, 60, 197
Wolstenholme Square 84, 85, 148, 176

World Discovery Centre 7, 16, 77
World Heritage Site 7, 16, 18, 31, 32
Writing on the Wall Festival 14, 182

X-Building 7

Year of City Life 16
Year of Creativity and Innovation 16
Year of Faith in One City 13, 169, 211
Year of Heritage 16
Year of Performance 16
Year of the Sea 14
Yellow Duckmarine 7, 211
Yellow Submarine 7

Ziba 7, 125

Index 224

LIVERPOOL EMPIRE THEATRE

Experience the best in large-scale entertainment at the **North West's Premier Theatre.** The Empire Theatre is the largest two-tier theatre in the UK with facilities ranked amongst the best in Europe. This spectacular touring venue offers everything from **Opera** and **Ballet** to **Comedy, Concerts** and **West End productions.** The theatre also boasts a three-tier glass atrium building which features wonderful facilities for conferences and events, and has magnificent views of the city.

For programme information call **ticketmaster** on **0870 606 3536**
Visit www.getlive.co.uk/liverpool

BLUECOAT
LIVERPOOL'S CENTRE FOR THE CONTEMPORARY ARTS

VISUAL ARTS
LIVE ART
MUSIC
DANCE
LITERATURE
PERFORMANCE
WORKSHOPS
EVENTS
SHOPS
CAFÉ
GARDEN

INFORMATION - 0151 709 5297
Building open Monday - Saturday 9.00am - 5.30pm

BOX OFFICE - 0151 707 9393
Box Office open Monday - Friday 11.00am - 4.00pm

Bluecoat, School Lane, Liverpool L1 3BX
www.bluecoatartscentre.com

NEPTUNE THEATRE
LIVERPOOL

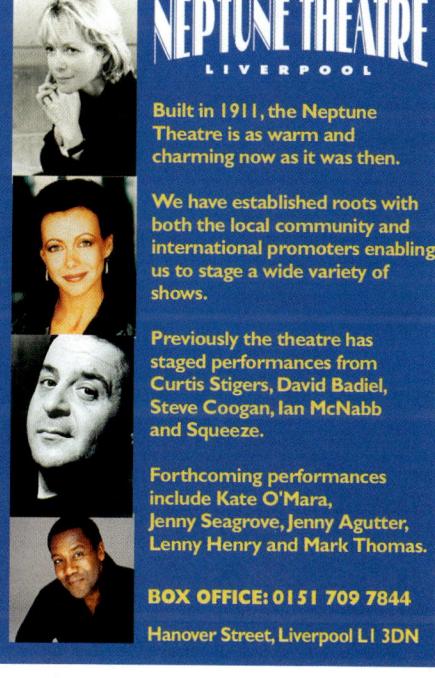

Built in 1911, the Neptune Theatre is as warm and charming now as it was then.

We have established roots with both the local community and international promoters enabling us to stage a wide variety of shows.

Previously the theatre has staged performances from Curtis Stigers, David Badiel, Steve Coogan, Ian McNabb and Squeeze.

Forthcoming performances include Kate O'Mara, Jenny Seagrove, Jenny Agutter, Lenny Henry and Mark Thomas.

BOX OFFICE: 0151 709 7844

Hanover Street, Liverpool L1 3DN

Ciao for now   226